PASSAGEWAY WEST

My Escape from East Germany

By: David J. Bloomfield

(As Told by Barbara Bloomfield)

My best to Claudia & Dara

Both

David Bloomfield

ISBN: 1-4107-1780-1 (e-book)
ISBN: 1-4107-1781-X (Paperback)

This book is printed on acid free paper.

1stBooks – rev. 02/08/03

To Shirley and Jeremy

Acknowledgement

I would like to thank Cathy Rusco at Muskegon Community College for providing the encouragement to keep on going.

CHAPTER I
Quedlinburg—Where Germany Began

Between philandering parents, war disruptions, personal misfortunes, and the reign of terror imposed by the Russians after the war, my only solace was derived from devotedly attached siblings. My brother, Erich, and sister, Rosel, were fifteen and fourteen years my elder.

I have been told that, according to German folklore, Barbara was the Patron Saint of the Artillery. I thought it quite appropriate that I should have received such a threatening name, considering my birth took place the day after Adolph Hitler's 49th birthday. At that time the thundering artillery of Hitler's army grew louder and more menacing throughout all of Europe. It may have merely been coincidental that my own story from the beginning has been one of turmoil and misadventures due, in some part, to the political and war crazed mind of the madman, Hitler himself.

1

Unfortunately, those of you born in the United States of America, have no concept of what growing up among war torn cities and occupying armies is remotely about. Not to say that those people living in Harlem, Watts, or even the inner cities of Detroit and Chicago, haven't faced horrendous obstacles; or that the southern blacks in the early 20th century didn't continually live in fear of their existence. My thoughts, however, as a seven-year-old child, spending night after night in the terror of a makeshift bomb-shelter beneath my house, while listening to earthshaking explosions above tearing apart my country, will remain with me always.

For the sake of you who think that the Old North Church in Boston is a touch of ancient history, I begin with the town of Quedlinburg, Germany, more than one thousand years older than the city of Boston. Here my life began. Comfortably nestled in the Harz Mountains, inside the triangle apexed by Magdeburg, Leipzig, and Kassel, in what was formerly considered the Deutsche Democratic Republic (East Germany), my city dates back to the year 545 AD. If you think that the landing of the Pilgrims at Plymouth Rock in 1620 is the beginning of history, I suggest you visit Eastern Europe. Remnants of the wall constructed to protect our city from invaders, by Heinrich I, in 922AD, when Quedlinburg was a province in Saxony, can still be seen. Children still climb on these ramparts with no knowledge that they are tampering with 1100 years of history. Interestingly enough, Heinrich I, commonly referred to in English speaking countries as Henry I, received the crown in 919AD as the first King of Germany in our historic city.

Quedlinburg is no ordinary Eastern European town. It is considered to be the cradle of German history. I write with great pride about my birthplace, as I still consider it my home, having spent the first 19 years of my life in this quaint but historic city. The half-timbered houses still stand after nearly 1000 years, two major wars, and a Russian occupation that permitted the entire infrastructure of Eastern Germany to disintegrate. At some point between the 10th and 12th century the city briefly became the capital of the Holy Roman Empire.

I first returned to Quedlinburg in 1971 with my 10-year-old daughter, Shirley; my first venture back following my escape from the East in 1957. Although it had fallen into a state of disrepair, I couldn't hold back the tears of joy as I walked the streets with Shirley showing her my childhood haunts, which I never expected to revisit under the current political regime. While there, the ever present and frightening Stasi followed us day and night from the moment we re-entered the East zone. A network of loyal East German Communists, the Stasi spent most of their time recruiting citizens to spy on their neighbors, friends, husbands, wives, parents, and anyone with whom they came in contact, in order to inform their secret police organization of any subversive thinking. Subversive, in East Germany, consisted of even hinting that something related to Communist rule could stand improvement. Such comments could send a citizen to jail permanently without the privilege of a trial or even the courtesy of informing relatives as to the cause or location of their disappearance.

King Henry, completely enamoured with Quedlinburg, now a city of only 25,000, made it the scene of the imperial diets and the seat of the courts of justice. Henry, his wife Mathilda, and Otto I, who founded the famous convent in Quedlinburg, are buried in the castle church, which even today is one of the more magnificent historic sights to grace Europe. It may also come as a shock to many that for more than 800 years, up until 1802, Quedlinburg was ruled entirely by women. The convent ruled the city and nearby fields while 39 abbesses ruled the convent during that period. My, how enlightened the Europeans were even then.

Although taking my daughter to see Quedlinburg was quite a thrilling experience, it paled in comparison to taking David, my American husband of 34 years at that time, to the place about which he had heard so much since we were married. Although he had traveled the world over on his numerous business trips, staying in suites at five star hotels, he had little difficulty acclimating himself to a tiny bedroom in the 250 year old Hotel Zum Baer. Its one public bathroom and shower on each floor and no elevator to carry us to our 3rd floor room proved to be only a slight inconvenience. The hotel, located in the center of the market square, goes back to the year 1230. It also served as the starting point of one of my childhood fantasies.

The charm of the Market Square, situated on the circumference of a half-mile circle of streets winding throughout the city, attracted teenagers from all over Quedlinburg. For those growing up in this city, tradition dictated that boys walk clockwise around the circle while their female companions, and those who they wished were companions, walk counter-clockwise. When meeting halfway around the circle, they would cordially introduce themselves, even though they may have been neighbors for years, and go off to have their ice cream and sodas together. My fantasy had always consisted of someday making this legendary walk with my husband, and now, after more than 50 years, it could happen.

The circle isn't a true circle, but a series of winding interconnecting streets starting with Breite Strasse, going to Bockstrasse, Heiligegeistrasse, and ending on Steinbrucke, which starts and completes the circle in front of the Zum Baer Hotel. There are a few streets intersecting the circle that caused the undoing of my much anticipated walk with David. After carefully explaining the route to him and virtually drawing him a picture indicating where to go, we went our opposite ways. Needless to say, he took one of the cross streets by mistake, and after walking over an hour on this planned 10-15 minute adventure, I finally discovered him hopelessly lost in a city small enough to walk every street in less than two hours. He did make one very interesting observation. He crossed Judengasse, Jewish Alley, one of the dark back streets, during his wanderings. The question arose as to why a street would be named after the religion that had been vilified in Germany for so many years, and whose very existence the German high command took such drastic measures to eliminate. Oddly enough, during our next visit to Quedlinburg, five years later, the Judengasse street sign had been obliterated, as it simply remained a dark, dingy alley with no name and, apparently, no hope of revival, based on its deteriorated condition.

Later, I proudly walked the original cobblestone streets dating back over 1000 years with him as we viewed the churches and statues built during the turn of the millenium. We walked on the walls built in the 12th century, designed to defend the city from robber barons and envious neighbors. To man all of the wall's outposts and watchtowers required 1400 men and women, an incredible number considering the population at that time was only 4000.

Finally, we arrived at the magnificent castle and convent built by Otto I. It recently made history with the discovery that an American soldier in 1945 had stolen some of the historical artifacts and treasures hidden in caves during the war to prevent theft and damage. He smuggled them back to Texas and, after his death, the German government had to pay three million dollars for their recovery. This was the castle in which I had spent so many hours of my youth playing with friends, and now is one of Europe's premier tourist attractions. I really hadn't anticipated the anguish that would overtake my feelings as so many memories of my past in this surrounding overwhelmed me. It was so difficult to make David understand how deeply I felt about revisiting this period, after accepting that it was a page in history that would never again be reopened.

CHAPTER II
House of Memories

Much of my early childhood and historical events of the war years, have been related to me by my brother, Erich, sister, Rosel, or my mother. Why not Dad? Hitler kept him busy as an officer in the army travelling from one battle front to another. In addition, his skills as a family communicator left much to be desired. He died during my mid-teens, and we had neither the time nor inclination to really converse with each other. He simply lacked the warm friendly personality I expected of a father. God knows what he would have said had he lived to see me marry an American Jew.

The framework and backdrop of my existence accounts for the turbulent plot leading me to my new life. It begins with my Mom's father, a cabinetmaker from a long line of cabinetmakers, starting with my grandfather's ancestors in the late 1500's. In those days, these skilled craftsmen commanded the same dignified respect as today's successful highly trained engineers or orthopedic surgeons. The Tangermann family of cabinet makers brought with it a house built in 1580 which stood in stature as one of the classics from 16th century for small German towns. A twenty-six room three-storied house large enough to shelter my grandfather, his family, and several apprentices working for him. Why it required five kitchens was well beyond my comprehension. When I try to imagine what my house has seen and done during its 420-year history, a separate biography of the structure alone would be appropriate. I'd call it "The Breite Strasse House."

One wing of the house actually connected to an old Jewish synagogue dating back 400 years, while behind it stood my grandfather's workshop where he stored his tools and raw wood for making cabinets.

I took David to see the house in 1994, and the two of us stood outside on the street on a warm summer's evening and marveled at the structure, both its history and stature. This half timbered building, on the corner of Breite Strasse and Schul-Strasse, had now been converted to a series of apartments, housing five or six different families. The beautiful courtyard, which once served as the garden and focal point for family gatherings, was now strewn with rubbish discarded by the East German oafs who were provided their shelter there by the generous dictatorship that passed as the government. This same government, by the way, confiscated the house after my family and I escaped through the minefields to the West. The synagogue had long been boarded up and, most likely, had not been used since prior to my being born. The Jewish population of Germany had been herded into camps where synagogues were of little use, with no one left to carry on the Jewish prayer rituals. Synagogues, therefore, had become obsolete.

As we walked through the courtyard, we could feel ourselves being suspiciously watched by the inhabitants from their windows, as though we were a threat to their existence. Walking from one set of windows to the next we felt their eyes scrutinizing our every move. How challenging it was to have grown up in East Germany, not knowing which of your friends, neighbors, or relatives would turn you in to the Stasi for uttering something even remotely related to your true political feelings. The air was heavy with suspicion of our presence and our American style clothing only contributed to their distrust.

We finally met an older lady who invited us in after I explained that she now lived my former home (and technically my present home). "Yes," I explained, "this is where I spent the first nineteen years of my life," while leaving unsaid, "and look how badly you people have messed it up." She informed us that the government was now considering the possibility of tearing the place down due to some mysterious indestructible fungus that seemed to have invaded the walls. Her real fear lay in the fact that I might be there to reclaim the house. Fat chance. Little did she realize that my life had taken on enough liabilities and needed no more entanglements like property ownership in East Germany.

As we exited the apartment, something on the outside porch caught my eye. An aluminum object shaped like a miniature rowboat, approximately five feet long and eighteen inches at it widest section. I called David over to show him my portable bathtub used by my mother to bathe me when I was a little girl. It wasn't "similar" to the tub; it *was* *the* tub, as I distinctly recall some of the markings. How strange to look at something so inanimate yet so personal that lived through the war, the Russian occupation, and now the liberation. A simple portable bathtub which, for the past 60 years, just hung around and watched it all happen after I left it behind for a different life thousands of miles away.

As we walked down the steps to leave, I couldn't help but remember the hiding place where my brother Erich used to wait for me to come down the stairs. He would jump out of the small alcove to scare the daylights out of me and laugh like hell when I screamed from sheer fright. Erich was truly different, but that's a story in itself that I will cover later.

Oddly enough, David and I returned again to my home five years later in 1999, only to discover that all of the tenants had been evicted and the main gate boarded up. We couldn't even walk into the courtyard or take one last look to see if my bathtub was still being stored outside the kitchen door, or whether they had closed off Erich's hiding place. I had lived there only nineteen years, and yet it felt as though all 420 years of the house's history were evaporating in front of me. As emotionally tied to my home as I am, I have no desire to return. My house had become an integral part of my family. Even today, because of that attachment, I feel very much the same way about the other houses in which I've lived. Maybe it all stems from the house on Breite Strasse, but my most avid passion has always been the beautification and embellishment of my home, both inside and out. My life today, to a large extent, is devoted to my garden and everything that blooms between the months of March and late November. It is an all consuming enthusiasm that occupies 60-70 hours a week during the growing months. During the winter I peruse every catalogue and gardening publication to enrich my knowledge of flowering plants to prepare for the arrival of spring. I keep an engraved stone at the entrance of my garden that reads: "An hour in the garden puts life's problems in perspective." David, of course, does the usual complaining when the bills arrive, but I simply explain that it certainly beats what we would be paying a therapist for the same peace of mind.

CHAPTER III

Ancestors—The Primal Cause

Not a lot can be said about my ancestors. My Mom's mother and father both died of cancer, he first of throat cancer, followed shortly thereafter by my grandmother of stomach cancer. Both were in their 70's, and considering that particular time and place in history, I'd say they lived a full life plus. My grandparents on my father's side both died before I was born, and since my father was not renowned for his communicative skills, I have virtually no knowledge of their personal history. I do recall my mother telling me that Grandpa Spannaus, an industrialist living in Aschersleben, roughly 60 kilometers from Quedlinburg, owned a number of flour mills and retail stores that sold the products from his mills. Today we would say that his business was "vertically integrated."

Without dwelling on my mother's childhood, I will only say that she must have been quite the unbridled young lady if her appetite for life prior to marriage was anything like it was after. Although my mother described herself as a "tom-boy," her sexual appetite later in life indicates she was anything but. The social structure in small German towns in the early 1900's seemed to revolve around structured settings such as chaperoned dances and tea parties. The dances were held in neighboring cities among the well-to-do families and served as the meeting place for those on the same social levels. As you may have surmised, that's how my Mom and Dad met.

After a rather lengthy courtship of two or three years, my mother became pregnant with Erich, my older brother. Unfortunately, this occurrence took place before they decided to marry, but the decision to wed was made shortly thereafter. Customarily, in those days, single moms were not expected to remain that way. Of course, the usual scandal associated with Grandma Tangermann's daughter having a child out of wedlock arose, and without even having to resort to the shotgun, my mother, Margarete Tangermann and father, Erich Spannaus were married during the summer of 1923. Such were the circumstances of their first "unwanted" child, Erich.

It was fortunate that my grandfather owned that large house in Quedlinburg, and that my mom was his favorite offspring due to her sparkling sense of humor, as it was about to receive two more inhabitants, my dad and his newborn son, my older brother, Erich. Remember that it also served as the home to my grandparents, my mother's sister, Agnes, and her husband, my great grandmother, and 10-15 apprentices who were employed by my grandfather, the cabinetmaker. The house did lose one resident shortly thereafter. My Aunt Agnes, who had been suffering from heart problems for some time, was warned by her doctor not to have any children; however, being part of the promiscuous Tangermann family she paid no heed to the warning. She gave birth to a baby boy and died of heart failure within the year.

Mom's sense of humor went beyond her willingness to tell stories and be the family prankster.

Her eyes held a contagious penetrating twinkle. You could actually see sparks dance between one corner of the eye to the other. This attribute may have served her quite well in later relationships. She also had the naiveté to believe in old wives tales, as she was told that a woman nursing a child, as she was with Erich, could not become pregnant. Thirteen months after Erich was born my mother delivered my older sister, Rosel, "unwanted" child number two. Not only an accident, but Rosel came at a time when additional family members were extremely difficult to afford. Germany in the late 1920's was experiencing the highest level of inflation that any country has ever witnessed in modern history. My mother often spoke of the time she went to buy a baby stroller for Erich one morning and discovered that she didn't have the 200,000DM in her purse to make the purchase. Having gone home to get more funds, she returned that afternoon to find the price had increased fifty per cent to 300,000DM. People were actually carrying money in large containers; the Deutsche Mark was so worthless.

My life, to a great extent, revolved around my mother, brother, and sister. My father, who died in 1953 when I was fifteen, spent a good deal of time between 1939 and 1945 being a good Wermacht officer doing his part to help the "Fatherland" conquer the rest of the free world. Being a strict disciplinarian, he brought the military formalities into his own home. Many were the times that I kissed him on the bald spot on top of his head, as Erich and Rosel shuddered, as they could never get away with such informalities. He apparently had a very short fuse and didn't hesitate to beat up on either of them for small infractions of his rules. Rosel took the brunt of the beatings that raised welts on her backside as Erich would hide until his anger cooled down.

When he took a Sunday stroll his eyes remained focused forward to the point that, if his own children were playing on the street outside of his narrow range of vision, there would be no sign of recognition. If my mother were entertaining a group of ladies for afternoon tea, they departed immediately when he appeared at the door. A man of intimidating demeanor.

To this day I like to think that my father really didn't believe in his mission for Hitler and acted in the capacity of the good soldier doing his job under duress. On the other hand, it is so difficult to truly understand the mentality of my family members during that period and what they actually knew of the horrors being carried on under their noses in the name of Deutschland Uber Alles. It was one thing to never have had the opportunity to question my father, but another to attempt to decipher my mother's cryptic answers when I was old enough to understand my country's history, and question her on the subject. In all good conscience, I would like to accept her response that she never knew of the horrors perpetrated in nearby concentration camps, but logic speaks differently.

I admit, however, that I have come across historical documents indicating that even German army officers, Field Marshal Von Rundstedt for one, were highly angered that the SS troops were demonstrating their courage exterminating defenseless civilians, particularly Polish Jews, instead of fighting the real war. He furthermore told the leader of the SS Task

Force in charge of the extermination process to evacuate the war zone, and that anti-Jewish measures taking place in Katowice (Aushwitz) would no longer be tolerated. A line of demarcation obviously existed between the Wehrmacht and the Nazis, who focused their efforts on the murder of all European Jews. My father hopefully sided with Von Rundstedt, but I will never know.

My father was born in the small town of Aschersleben, 60 kilometers from Quedlinburg in 1900, into a family of millers. With both the Tangermann and Spannaus families grounded in old money, it was not surprising that Margarete and Erich should become acquainted, particularly in the "old" country where class segregation is considered second only to religious classification. Being the 3rd of four boys he learned very early that privileges go to those who don't break the rules. Having gotten my mother pregnant before marriage, he confined his early adulthood to working for his father while attending school locally. His better behaved older brothers were fortunate enough to be sent to Heidelberg for their education.

So Grandfather Spannaus had four boys. Now if you lived in any other country in the world, or, for that matter, even on some other planet, it wouldn't be difficult to surmise that a family assigning names like Guenther, Hans, Erich, and Kurt must be living in the neighborhood of the German Republic. Guenther, the oldest, managed several of his father's retail bakeshops, and keeping within the class stratification, married a wealthy Protestant woman. They later moved to Berlin in the late 1920's, a move that had been motivated by their growing support of the National Socialist German Workers' party (NSDAP), under the guidance of a lunatic by the name of Adolph Hitler. Uncle Guenther and Aunt Clare became devoted supporters of this deranged madman.

CHAPTER IV
Dictator of Death

Adolph Hitler had a profound effect upon my life, the life of my family, and for that matter, the entire world. Although the world population had been strongly influenced by this "patched-together rabble-rouser who ghastly distorted history," in the words of Thomas Mann, it is important to understand that it was my family and I who lived within the borders of his dictatorship. There was no escaping from the havoc he wreaked upon my home and my life. In looking back, I try to imagine what logic or emotion attracts basically good people to such an evil philosophy. I still question where my loyalties would have been residing, had I been an adult living between 1920 and 1945.

Born the son of a minor Bavarian customs official and peasant woman, he never even finished high school. He felt compelled not only to bend the world to his will, but also to decimate an entire religious population at the same time. His talents as an artist were so limited that he was twice refused admittance to the Vienna Academy of Fine Arts. During his years of failure, he developed, through various reading materials, a strong anti-Semitic philosophy. This led him to believe and pontificate upon the fact that Germany's ills during the depression were created by Jewish capitalism, Communism, the Treaty of Versailles, and Social Democrats. Ultimately, six million Jews were exterminated based upon these beliefs.

Hitler served as a private in the Bavarian army during WW I. Although never even considered for a promotion, he became elected as the party chairman of the National Socialist Workers (Nazi) Party in 1921, seventeen years before I was born. Can you imagine the gullibility and hopeless desperation of the German people to make such a senseless choice? Apparently, according to my mother, his ability to speak so emotionally to the masses looking for leadership, was so charismatic, that the German people believed in what he said and would have followed him through a wall of fire, which many did.

In 1923, the year my brother Erich was born, Germany faced economic chaos. The 300,000DM that my mother spent for the baby stroller may have been worth fifty US dollars in the evening, but earlier in the day its cost of 200,000DM was also equivalent to the same fifty dollars. Hitler took the opportunity to lead an uprising in Munich against the Weimar Republic, but spent nine months in jail for his troubles. During his imprisonment he wrote Mein Kampf, the guiding influence on a population destined for self-destruction. Keep in mind that this was my Uncle and Aunt's hero. Yes, he could be described as one of the most politically astute dictators of all time. When the Great Depression struck in 1929, while blaming it on the Jews and Communists, he attracted an increased following, eventually leading to his appointment as Chancellor in 1933. Truly exciting and unusual times led up to my birth five years later. One man had set the stage for the climate of my future.

Once in power, Hitler declared himself dictator and established his secret police, the Gestapo, to eliminate any opposition. He vowed to create a master race of Aryans, while ruthlessly persecuting the Jewish population to gain the people's support.

I still find it difficult to understand how both Uncle Guenther and his wife, Clare, became devoted supporters of this madman. But then again, being only a young child, I never remembered listening to Hitler speak.

With the aid of propaganda chief, Goebbles, he convinced the vast majority of the German population, including Uncle Guenther, that this hate philosophy was justified, and the only remedy meant creating a race of pure Aryans. My mother often spoke of how intently the population listened to his speeches and how masterfully he motivated them to perform such evil. So loyal to this belief was Guenther that he and Clare agreed to have no children in order to devote their lives to supporting Hitler.

I say that the Goebble's propaganda machine influenced the majority of the German population as opposed to all of it, as my brother became the classic rebel during that period. Erich at 15, when Hitler was preparing for his invasion of Czechoslovakia, declaring the Treaty of Versailles null and void, was sent to Berlin to live with Uncle Guenther; a temporary move to get him out of the way while my mother attempted to abort me.

Under Uncle Guenther's influence it became evident to an artistic, music loving, well read, gentle soul such as Erich, that Hitler would bring about the ultimate demise of a great country, his own. Erich, at the tender age of 16, predicted Germany's collapse and visibly displayed his feelings to a critical Guenther during the parade in Berlin celebrating Hitler's 49th birthday. When he showed a distasteful lack of respect for the proceedings, and in fact a defying contempt for anything associated with militarism and Hitler, he was severely rebuked by my loyal Uncle and Aunt. Meanwhile, during his stay with Guenther and Clare, Erich had no knowledge of the fact that my mother was attempting to erase my existence.

My "loving and caring" Nazi Tante Clare provided me with some lasting memories of my early childhood that still remain with me for good reason. Maybe it's just easier to recall the evil than the good in people. Tante Clare was truly Hitler's version of the Aryan purist, tall, attractive, hair pulled back in a bun and probably capable of being a prison guard at Treblinka or Auschwitz.

At the age of three I became quite ill with stomach cramps one night when my parents were having a party at our home. My constant crying disrupted the party and Mother came into the bedroom to determine the problem and soothe my pain. She picked me up in her arms, rocked me, put a pacifier between my teeth, and started singing a lullaby.

At that point, and after a few glasses of wine, Clare stormed into the bedroom, ripped the pacifier from my mouth, grabbed me from my mother's arms, and crudely tossed me into my crib. In no uncertain terms she told my mother, "This is not how a good German girl should be raised. You must be very strict and never pamper her." When my crying resumed after being thrown in the crib, she grabbed my mother's arm, led her out of the room, and turned out the light before slamming my bedroom door shut. This, of course, from a woman who had no children of her own and had devoted her entire existence to Hitler. To this day, I can still visualize her from my crib playing the role of the Aryan teacher as one of my few visions of early childhood.

So preoccupied was this devoted couple to the Nazi Party that, with Clare's encouragement, Guenther paid less and less attention to his shops and more and more to his climbing ascendance within the Party. Eventually he became such an important official within the regime's political structure, that he and his wife made a suicide pact in 1945 to be carried out if Germany were to be defeated. As it turned out, only Clare kept her end of the bargain. Guenther somehow managed to escape detection and proceeded to live out the remainder of his life as a normal German citizen, disappearing into the fabric of German society with all of the other Nazi fanatics who strangely enough simply vanished.

One of my last and possibly only personal memories of Guenther took place shortly after the war. As a seven-year-old I recall that the Americans occupied Quedlinburg at the time. Our house, which consisted of three stories and several rooms on each floor, was more than I, as a youngster, could hope to fully utilize. The floor plan of the second level looked more like a disfigured maze than a planned layout, unlike today's more modern homes. With the house located on the corner each of the four bedrooms faced one of the intersecting streets. On one side of the house were three adjoining bedrooms connected by a common bathroom and hallway. On the other side across the hall and through the bathroom my father's study and adjoining bedroom overlooked Schulstrasse.

When my mother put certain rooms off limits to me, it presented no loss of my freedom to roam about the remainder of the house. Not even curious as to why the door to my father's study was always shut, I played only in those rooms made available to me. This may also have been a function of the times in which we lived when curiosity could prove to be very dangerous.

A great commotion going on in the street outside our house one rainy afternoon got my attention. I could hear the noise from my room on the other side of the house. In my attempt to determine the cause of this disturbance, I ran through the bathroom down the hallway to the opposite side of the house to look out the window of my father's study. This meant that, without thinking, I barged through the forbidden door to gain access to the view. Upon opening the door, I stopped in my pursuit as though I had run into a brick wall.

There, sitting in one of my father's favorite chairs, with a cigarette dangling from his lower lip, an elderly bearded man glared at me. His surprise at my intrusion appeared to exceed my own. The deep wrinkles in his face were partially covered by a scraggly unshaven gray growth that reminded me of a hobgoblin from one of Grimm's fairy tales. What hair that remained on his head hadn't been brushed or combed in weeks and the robe he wrapped himself in contained the drippings of his last few meals surrounded by holes burned by the

35

falling cigarette ashes. I was introduced to Uncle Guenther!

I faced a very stern looking man sitting erect in Pappi's leather chair clothed only in his bathrobe. He gave no sign of recognition and didn't bother to even acknowledge his seven-year-old niece. He certainly resembled my father, but the events of the past several years and his association with criminals and murderers had obviously taken its toll. If I knew then what I know now, I would have turned my back and walked out. Being naïve, however, I tried to hug him, as a child would normally do with a relative, but would have received more warmth from a granite statue than I did from my Uncle Guenther.

Apparently he had escaped Berlin, with his name on the Allied list of high ranking Nazis and somehow made his way back to Quedlinburg. Finding my mother living there with Rosel, Erich, and myself, he insisted that my mother take him in to hide from the occupying forces. With my father in a British prison camp somewhere in Europe, and no other men in the house to help protect her three children, my mother agreed.

Upon making this surprise discovery, my mother took me aside and very sternly warned me that I was not to breathe a word of Guenther's presence to anyone. She stressed that if the American soldiers, who were then occupying Quedlinburg, were to find out about his hiding in our house we might all be put to death. Still, the news to a seven-year-old of this clandestine arrangement was quite exciting, and in less than an hour I had excitedly informed my friends that my father had returned and now had a beard. As the word of my indiscretion spread quickly, that evening Guenther left the house and eventually made his way to Bavaria and suffered through a rather painful bout with lung cancer before dying. In retrospect, my big mouth was probably more beneficial to the family than harmful.

Not all of my uncles fell so helplessly under the influence of the German Führer. Hans, four years younger than Guenther, moved to Kalbe, not far from Quedlinburg, and opened up a series of men's fashion stores. He apparently got through the war period without a great deal of misfortune, however my brother and sister, from whom I have derived much of my information, eventually lost track of him.

My own brother, Erich, seemed to have inherited the characteristics of Kurt, the youngest of the four. Kurt, the artist and dreamer was considered the most handsome of the four boys, and certainly the most talented, playing both the piano and violin, in addition to his artistic abilities. His talents reflected the nature of many of Germany's best and brightest who were sent to battle to satisfy the crazed ego of one man. Kurt joined the many thousands of German youths that were sacrificed on the Russian front in 1941 and never returned. My own personal recollections of that side of the family were the two daughters of Kurt and Friedchen Spannaus. They were Ute and Rotraud, who I clearly remember when they came to visit and we played in the public sandbox in a nearby park.

Living in Germany during the 1920's and 1930's can only be described as riding a roller coaster without knowing that the ride would ever end. It meant living through periods of war, demagoguery, political instability, periods of mass inflation and major recessions. Having not been party to this myself, I have only read and listened to my family about what the Spannaus's and Tangermann's survived. It was during one such period of near depression that caused my grandfather to lose his flour business. Because my mother's family had generous resources, they were able to keep their daughter afloat by loaning her husband enough money to get into the steel warehousing economy.

Just think of joining the world of steel during the 1930's in Germany. With Hitler gearing up to wage war on all of Europe and, eventually, the rest of the free world, the country was in dire need of planes, ships, armaments, tanks, and every other conceivable product derived from steel. My, how fortuitous. My family was restored to their former economic status with the help of the Tangermann wealth. It should also be mentioned that not too many years later, many American families achieved considerable riches in the steel business reaping obscene profits through the "gray market" economy. Choosing between patriotism and wealth was not a difficult decision for many in the steel warehousing and distribution business.

It pains me to continue referring to the guiding political and economic influence of that period, Adolph Hitler. He virtually dictated the future events that affected my entire family and me. In 1938, the year I was born, Hitler outwardly demonstrated his dissatisfaction with the Treaty of Versailles and the humiliating defeat of Germany in World War I. He was determined to expand Germany's borders and provide living space (Lebensraum), toward the east. He proceeded by marching his troops into the Sudetenland in Czechoslovakia five months after I was born. Hitler's world terrorism had commenced and from that time on, my father, a colonel in the German army, became a sometime visitor to our home.

My brother still reminds me of Kristallnacht or Crystal Night, the Night of Broken Glass, which Hitler decreed two months after Germany's occupation of Czechoslovakia, and seven months into my life. Throughout Germany mobs were incited to destroy any synagogues, buildings, or stores remotely connected to

Jewish owners or sympathizers. Even in Quedlinburg the citizens did their duty smashing Jewish storefronts while attempting to burn the only synagogue. History records that these thugs demolished thousands of Jewish homes, stores, and synagogues and the Jews were then ordered to clean up the mess and pay a fine of one billion marks to be paid out of their confiscated property.

CHAPTER V
Birth of a Survivor

Now that we have established a reasonable setting of a country in turmoil along with the background of those most critical in my life, my parents and ancestors, we have arrived at my entrance to this chaos. It started with an innocent christening of Uncle Hans's son, Achim. Hans, you recall, had moved to Kalbe, and doing quite well as the owner of men's fashion stores. He invited my mother and father to the christening. Since the railroad system in Germany ran with such great efficiency and encompassed so many locations, Mom and Dad took the train to Kalbe for the occasion.

As was customary at such affairs, it was not unusual for alcohol consumption to pre-empt the christening itself. My mother and father were no exceptions and did their share of imbibing. I suspect that they anticipated their activities ahead of time, which accounts for their taking a train such a short distance. I would also suspect this was the reason for making a reservation in the sleeping car for the return trip to Quedlinburg. It was on the return trip in a state of non-sobriety that I was conceived.

Keep in mind, I had a brother, Erich, and sister, Rosel, 15 and 14 years old at that time. My parents were in their late thirties, a somewhat dangerous age to bear children in those days, and my mother had previously given birth to a stillborn after carrying nine months. As a matter of fact, she carried the stillborn quite some time after it had died because the doctors couldn't induce labor due to some sort of blood poisoning. I'm not sure whose blood was poisoned. My mother was quite ill with her own blood poisoning for nearly a year following that experience. She was warned not to have any more children, but who pays any attention to such drivel when whiskey and sex are involved?

My mother's mom was truly upset and considered the pregnancy an act of total irresponsibility. Her mother proceeded to locate an abortionist a few blocks away. Fortunately, the abortionist, not being medically trained, botched the procedure. Apparently, the use of knitting needles were as dangerous then as they are today. This, of course, serves as only one testimony in support of legalizing abortion, so that such butchers and hacks are put out of business. The outcome, of course, was my coming into the world of the Third Reich during its period of greatest unrest. Thus begat "unwanted" child number three, Barbara.

My mother truly did not need the aggravation of another child at this point in her life and certainly not during the overall period of political uncertainty. Although my name corresponded to that of the Patron saint of the Artillery, my parents decided that they would call me by the much softer name of Barbel. Mommy often commented on the fact that I was her only child born in a hospital, as both Erich and Rosel's deliveries took place in the confines of the house on Breite Strasse.

No one informed my father of the attempted abortion until it became evident, and he railed against my mother and grandmother in anger. His emotions, of course, were not related to his position on pro-life or pro-choice. He felt that a new baby might add some sunshine into a life that had become rather drab and unpleasant, considering what the German people suffered through at that time. He told my mother, after discovering what had happened that he would have divorced her had the so-called abortionist been successful.

Some people have been blessed by the gods of good fortune smiling upon them from the time they exit the womb, while others spend their entire life seeking those gods' approval and acceptance. I fell into the category of the unblessed. In the normal discipline of those born to good German stock, tradition allowed newborn children to cry in a hospital setting until they virtually choked on their own tears. It would be considered a sign of spoiling the child if a nurse actually attempted to lift up the baby to determine that something so mundane as a diaper pin pierced their buttocks or rampant fever had exploded in their brain.

Yes, the good German nurses, many of whom would probably have also made outstanding concentration camp guards, did not want to spoil me. They ignored my endless crying, from the moment of birth throughout the entire first night. After all, being born under the portent of artillery thunder, I might grow up to be a weak sister if someone happened to come to my aid. By a stroke of "good fortune" the blood emanating from my body finally discolored the bedding that encased me. At that point one of my mother's friends, while visiting the ward, picked me up to find my entire basket filled with bloody sheets caused by severe intestinal bleeding. The nurses told my mother that she could not see me until my condition had improved and that my chances of survival approached 50-50. Not bad odds for a horse race, but disastrous when betting on one's life. Even today my brother, Erich, blames my sickly condition on the failed attempt to abort me.

When presented to Mother shortly after my birth, she recalled that my complexion was an abnormally healthy looking pink, which gave rise to my nickname, "Marzipan Baby." They wouldn't permit her to feed me while I stayed in isolation for eight days. Eight days during which my mother remained in a state of complete depression, not even being informed of my status. Eight days of continuous blood transfusions that apparently saved my frail life.

Finally, on the ninth day after my birth, one of the more sympathetic nurses came to my mother's room with a bouquet of flowers, and using the endearing form of her name, said, "Gretchen, your daughter wants to feed today." This news, of course, put my mother into a state of hysterics, having heard nothing about my condition for over a week. After a number of sedatives she finally settled down, and upon gazing at a very shriveled, thin, undernourished baby, who no longer could claim the Marzipan nickname, questioned whether or not they had presented her with the same Barbel. My animation and fierce kicking gave her hope. Yes indeed, I was a survivor and will continue to be for the remainder of my life.

After providing Erich some lame excuse for his being carted off to live with his Nazi uncle, Mommy summoned him home and he happily took the first available train from Berlin back to Quedlinburg. When my mother greeted him with the news of my birth, every bone in his frail body reflected his ecstatic response as he danced and jumped around the train depot with uncontrollable joy about having a baby sister. My truly sensitive brother that is still there for me today. The circumstances have changed, however, as he now suffers in a nursing home with crippling arthritis, and a body covered with the rashes of psoriasis. He remains a virtual invalid, and I am the one who must be there for him.

While it would seem most improbable that two misfortunes could occur during the first six months of my existence, fate turned on me again. With my father off on some military assignment, Rosel began to feel like the mature 15-year-old that she deeply desired to be. One of her favorite pastimes consisted of putting me into the baby carriage and wheeling me around the city to get both of us some fresh mountain air. Of course, at the tender age of five months I knew nothing about fresh air or her true motives. Her walk with me simply served an excuse to get out of the house and secretly rendezvous with her most recent male acquaintance. Probably one she had encountered on the famous "circle walk."

Boiling milk before putting it in the baby bottle served as the sterilization process in those days. After putting the hot milk in the bottle, a cork covered the bottle before the nipple was placed on top. Rosel, in trying to impress her new boyfriend, chose to use me as the instrument. By teasing me with the bottle filled with hot milk and waving it in front of my face, she displayed her true ignorance of the laws of physics. The pressure blew off the cork and nipple, shooting the scalding hot milk all over my face. The shouting and screaming attracted my mother who ran out of the house, picked me up, and with Rosel, carried me to the doctor at the end of Bahnhof Strasse next to the train station.

While waiting for the doctor to treat me, Rosel lingered outside the office on the bridge over the Bode River, which passed through the city. Apparently, she spent the entire time there debating with herself whether or not to jump. Fortunately, she chose to live.

It must have been a terrible sight to behold, as my mother later told me, that with my face and upper body covered with huge blisters, I looked like some outer space creature. One at a time the doctor drained the blisters and proceeded to wrap my entire face in bandages, leaving an opening for one eye, my nostrils, and my mouth. Although I was smiling then, I still feel the results of the permanent damage to my right eye and the scars under my chin 64 years later. For the second time I had proven my ability to survive during a lifetime of such challenging opportunities.

I often wished that my athletic conditioning had made me immune to the hurtful experiences that continually plagued me. Pain seemed to follow me at every turn. At the age of seven I developed a middle ear infection that felt like fireworks exploding inside my brain. As little as I remember of my childhood, the agony associated with those experiences stand out. Hospitalized, they kept me in a room where I could only look through the glass to see Rosel and my mother waving to me. Later I recall being held down by four nurse's aides since anesthetics were scarce and reserved for military personnel. I remember the excruciating pain encountered while the doctor stuck something in my ear to help cure the infection. To this day, I shudder whenever anyone even comes close to touching my left ear for any reason.

CHAPTER VI
War's Devastation

On Sept 1st, 1939, five months after my first birthday, Germany proceeded to decimate their neighbor, Poland; exactly one year after Hitler and his gang had taken over Austria and the Sudetenland, promising, as part of the Munich Pact, that there would be no more aggression. Still agonizing over the "bad deal" Germany got through the Treaty of Versailles, he seemed determined to regain the land they relinquished in 1918 and impose German rule on Poland while annihilating every enemy of Nazism.

Try to visualize the life of my family and the chaos to which they were subjected, as my father conducted Hitler's war less than 200 miles from our home. Not just a war, but a blitzkrieg, lightning war, where they burned entire Polish villages and rounded up civilians by the thousands before summarily slaughtering them. Two wars, in fact, were being waged in Poland: one against the Polish army, and an even more intense war against the Polish citizens, primarily Jews. As their homes were burned, and the children attempted to flee from the rubble, they were massacred. Thousands of women and children with no idea what was going on were herded to the central market places to be lined up and executed. According to the diary of one German officer, "it was the Fuhrer's intention to exterminate the entire Polish nation." An integral part of that objective involved the annihilation of all Jews of Europe. By the end of September Poland surrendered. Historians later disclosed that more than ten thousand teachers, doctors, priests, and local business people had been corralled and murdered, not including the hundreds of thousands of Jews sent to their deaths in the concentration camps. That number expanded to six million by the end of the war.

Yes, there were minor protests by some of the German citizens, and even by a few of the military officers concerning the conduct of the war. I'm not certain that my family participated in those protests, as the threat of deportation to the concentration camps that were being established, hung as a heavy cloud over their heads. Even members of a platoon of German soldiers couldn't resist protesting to their superiors upon witnessing an SS detachment march twenty Jewish Polish children under the age of ten to a nearby cemetery and shoot them. Hitler's response; a tirade about this not being a war "to be fought by the Salvation Army." I can only hope that my own father would have been among the objectors.

Not that a history lesson about World War II is in order, but today as I look at photographs taken by my father meticulously dated with notes of their locations, I can retrace his whereabouts and movements as I progressed through the very early years of my infancy. Although I have no pictures or evidence of his being part of the Polish blitzkrieg, his presence was quite evident as Hitler turned his efforts towards Luxembourg, Belgium, and Holland when attempting to conquer France and the Low Countries.

Even the dates on his photographs correspond with Hitler's attack on Belgium and the Netherlands in May of 1940, shortly after my second birthday. My father posed on his horse, as good German cavalry officers normally do when having their picture taken, while the handwriting on the picture only stated "May 1940-Belgium." It said nothing about how the German juggernaught proceeded to destroy the cities and populations of Rotterdam, Antwerp, and Brussels on their way the North Sea. As a matter of fact, the next photos show him resting in Antwerp, followed by one of him standing next to a large body of water that can only be the North Sea itself.

I really find it quite intriguing seeing and imagining what was taking place through the eyes of my father during my formative years. I look at pictures of him today with his troops milling around in front of a department store in Brussels or of him and his officer friends standing by the bahnhof in Antwerp. And there they are again riding their horses next to the bombed out ruins of some nondescript church in Flanders. The album contains picture after picture of the Low Countries with virtually none of the civilians who would normally be doing their daily business on these bright sunny afternoons. I guess for the people of

Belgium, France and the Netherlands, these days weren't so bright and sunny. Even though I have few recollections of my youth, I can at least see what my father was doing when I was two or three years old.

In less than one month the German army trekked the 150 miles from their border to the coastal cities of northern France and Belgium. By mid-June of 1940, Hitler had conquered most of Europe. From looking at my father's pictures of ruins and statues, it appeared as though his army seemed more interested in the tourist aspects of the conquest than the battle itself. This particular campaign, at least for my father, appears to have ended in Paris. There he took the opportunity to photograph a number of pictures of the Arch de Triumph and the Eiffel Tower.

I'm not certain how long my father remained in France; however, I know that Hitler turned his attention towards the Balkans in the summer of 1941, just after I turned three years old. According to Erich, Pappi's involvement with the fighting in Yugoslavia nearly resulted in his capture and imprisonment had he not been fortunate enough to quietly escape across the border to Austria during that campaign. He would certainly have died in a prison camp operated by the Yugoslavian resistance movement.

I then came across some photographs in his collection corresponding to the period shortly after my third birthday, June of 1941. Hitler had launched a massive attack on his old friend Stalin. In attempting to defeat Russia, and take possession of the oil fields of the Caucasus, Hitler spared no resources and moved more than three million German troops, including my father, to the Russian front. These pictures don't display quite the leisurely attitude as the ones from Paris. Now the German soldiers, bundled up in their warmest winter uniforms on snow covered terrain, are pushing vehicles out of what were formerly roads that the Russian winter had converted to sludge filled swamps. Apparently Hitler looked at a Russian victory to be accomplished in a matter of two or three months. He certainly would have liked to have conquered Moscow and the Caucuses before the Russian winter set in.

How depressing to look at pictures he took of his comrades in arms pushing ambulances filled with wounded soldiers out of the swampy roads made impassable by the heavy autumn rains. The Russian troops as well as the weather had obviously disrupted Hitler's time schedule. I can see the battle ruins of snow covered farmhouses in the desolate frozen Russian countryside and pictures of my father in Minsk where they had taken 300,000 Russian prisoners and from Smolensk where they captured another 300,000 Russians. I couldn't find many photographs taken after the Russian winter set in when Stalin had mounted his counter-offensive. It became apparent that the German army now focused on defending itself as the temperature dropped like a stone. The snow drifted and neither their equipment nor their winter outfits could prevent the severe cold from overwhelming them. The trucks and tanks froze in place and there seemed to be no will to fight or even take photographs. Hitler ordered my father's battalion to stand fast on December 18th 1941. He instructed them not to retreat to Poland even as they suffered under the pounding of the Russian counter-attack. Father lost many of his troops during the winter of 1941, however, they remained strong enough to ultimately withstand that winter and continue their assault toward Stalingrad and the Caucasus in the summer of 1942. It still seems hard for me to believe that I was part of a nation conducting total war on all borders of our country, and my family talked so little about it, even after the war had ended. What an unusual way to grow up.

There don't seem to be any pictures dated after July of 1942, when Stalin issued his orders "Not a step back," which seemed to have mustered all of the strength available in each Russian soldier to protect the Motherland. As my father and his men were forced to retreat, it marked the beginning of the end for the German army. By this time the Americans and British were fully involved in the war, and I was now old enough to remember the sound of air raid sirens and bombs exploding. I no longer needed the pictures taken by my father to know that the German people were fighting for their lives and we, in our defenseless homes, were at the mercy of American and British bombers.

During the summer of 1943 I had just turned five when the continual bombing, in efforts to destroy German factories, destroyed the cities of Hamburg and Schweinfurt. The Russians had now taken the offensive and began pushing my father and his troops back towards the border. The Americans, in the meantime, had made plans to invade the European continent at Normandy, France, and Hitler, in anticipating the invasion, moved a massive amount of his army including my father to the French coast to greet the invasion.

As history has well documented, June of 1944 marked the invasion of Europe by the Americans and British at Normandy. There they captured my father and held him prisoner until the war ended a year later. Even at six years old when the invasion took place, my mother failed to inform me of what was happening. My country under siege from both directions, the Russians storming through the Balkans squeezing us from the east, and the Americans and British racing through France and Belgium pushing us from the west. 1944 became a year of continual bombing with one city after another crumbling from the British bomber raids that took place nearly every night. Meanwhile, V-2 rockets rained down on England in retaliation, causing thousands of lives to be lost on both sides. Our small family tried to go about doing our daily living under this threat.

I personally remember very little about World War II, other than the fact that I rarely saw my father and never knew that something called "war" could be so devastating. Considering that the bloodshed raged between my first and seventh birthday, it really isn't very surprising that my memory recalls only that which took place in the latter years. But what memories those are.

Quedlinburg, innocently located in the southern part of the scenic Harz Mountains, happened to be dangerously close to the city of Nordhausen, another city dating back to the year 1000 in a region of magnificent beauty, tradition, and magical folklore. The southern Harz created the seeds for flowers and plants exported all over the world designed to beautify the gardens from America to Asia. What a contrast, turning such a peaceful setting into a target for English and American weapons of destruction when the bombs started to fall.

In Nordhausen the Nazi high command had established the largest underground V-2 rocket plant in Germany. The German masterminds were also clever enough to provide their own source of slave labor for this operation by locating one of their most notorious concentration camps within the Nordhausen complex. How very brilliant, to satisfy the economics of war by supplying free labor at the expense of annihilating an entire religion, forcing them to create the weapons to be used against those that were in fact trying to save them.

Many prisoners lived underground during the V-2 production, and never saw the light of day during the remainder of their lives, which in most cases turned out to be a few short years. Fortunately for us, the military had located their launching base at

Peenemunde, an island in the Baltic Sea on the border between Poland and Germany.

Once the Allied forces had discovered Nordhausen's secret, the bombing started with a vengeance. In fact, more than fifty percent of the entire city of 46,000 people was decimated. Why are my memories so vivid? Try to imagine being six years old getting ready for bed every night listening to the sound of air raid sirens. This was followed by my being dragged to a basement bomb shelter shuddering with fear surrounded by mature adults frightened out of their wits. We could hear the planes roaring overhead and the explosions taking place less than thirty miles from my home. Occasionally planes would get lost, or not be able to locate their target, and my neighborhood would suffer their error. To this day, my heart still beats a little faster, and my skin generates goose bumps at the sound of any sirens, whether to announce the noon hour or an ambulance on the way to an emergency. A warning to which one never becomes accustomed.

The bomb shelter initially served as our family wine cellar. We crawled down there without lights among the potatoes, coal, and racks of my father's wine collection. Once there, someone usually lit a single candle so they could see if all were accounted for. During my first return visit to Quedlinburg with David, I pointed out the stairway leading to that cellar. It had been sealed. Erich, even today, reminds me of my terror as I prayed during the air raids for the safety of my family.

On occasion the raids came during the daylight hours, and we were directed to go to the bunkers located under the school.

Some of the soldiers fighting in the German army were Yugoslavs sent to our region. As the bombs continued to rain down day after day and night after night, the Yugoslav soldiers sometimes crowded into the school bunkers with us.

Finally, after months of going through the nightly routine in the cellar, we heard some strange sounding voices one morning calling outside in a foreign language. "Get out!" One by one we crawled over the coal and potatoes petrified of what lay ahead. Cautiously I took each cellar step towards the fresh air into the blinding sunlight. After being herded from the cellar and ordered to put our hands high over our heads, I discovered that I had wet my pants and never even knew when. For years we had listened to the tales about the evil Americans. Now we were about to come face to face with these heartless monsters.

It would be difficult for anyone who has not seen the ravages of war first hand to even comprehend what mental gymnastics twist through the mind of a six-year-old. The American citizen has not witnessed a war in his own backyard since the late 1860's, when the Civil War crashed down upon them. This means that those living in America today simply can't conceive the feelings and emotions of the children in Bosnia, Vietnam, Israel, or particularly all of Europe between 1939 and 1945. A foreign invader had come to my home with weapons of destruction and pointed those weapons at my family and myself, speaking in a language that I never even imagined possible to comprehend.

We emerged from the cellar with our hands high above our heads, and watched helplessly as our neighbors came forth from their respective hiding places on Breite Strasse. I remember looking around at my neighborhood, my hands raised and pants wet with fear, only to see broken windows, strangers in uniforms with rifles, and 30-40 neighbors all cowering under the fear of the ruthless American guns. The men living in our neighborhood, mostly those too old to be sent to fight for the Fatherland, were ordered to kneel down.

I then heard a noise that to this day haunts my worst nightmares. Very faintly I could hear a soft rumbling off in the distance, which sounded, at first, like storm clouds just beginning to gather their thunder. Gradually, it grew somewhat louder, as though the storm was growing in intensity. The louder it grew the less it seemed like thunder, and the more it felt like the threat of destruction. I looked up and saw, almost as if in a dream, a huge cannon, even before seeing the tank to which it was mounted, rounding the corner entering Breite Strasse. The rumbling of a convoy of Sherman tanks approaching over cobblestones, laid down over 1000 years ago, was enough to send many of us into a state of frozen terror.

When the huge mounted gun appeared swinging around the corner of Grabengasse onto Breite Strasse, I had no idea of what type of monster was approaching. I only know from the fright exhibited by the adults crowded next to me on the street, that it was something to fear. The procession of tanks rolled toward the Market Square with the space between vehicles occupied by German soldiers with their hands held high in the air. My recollection of sounds includes the voices of whimpering adult civilians to whom we were looking for support, and the rumbling noise of those fierce machines.

I recently saw the movie, *The Saving of Private Ryan.* In one of the more dramatic scenes I again heard that familiar sound of the tanks on cobblestone. The sound, with all of the memories it revived from more than 50 years ago, so terrified me during the movie that I had to get up and leave the theater.

As the American tanks rolled toward the town center and five of us young children stood in a state of terror, one of the American soldiers apparently recognized our distress and offered me a stick of gum. Of course, not knowing what it was, I could only stand there and stare at it, while he proceeded to show me how to eat it by unwrapping a piece for himself, putting it in his mouth and demonstrating the chewing process. My brother, the unceasingly hungry Erich, became quite jealous, as he was too old to be treated as a child to be soothed with chewing gum.

Having lived in America now for quite some time, it seems that the children born in the 1930's fed on a steady diet of war movies during their youth. Some based on the battles in the Pacific against the Japanese, like *Thirty Seconds Over Tokyo* or *The Sands of Iwo Jima*, while others focused on Europe such as *Battleground*, or even *Sergeant York* going back to the First World War. Hollywood glamorized war with the likes of John Wayne, Gary Cooper, William Bendix, and a host of other Hollywood immortals. I never saw this thrilling chapter of film making history, with its allure for excitement where the "good guys always win," until much later in my life. I can say very confidently, however, that being a confused child in the middle of this plight was not quite the same as it was portrayed in the cinema.

While American youngsters visualized war as German soldiers being decimated with hand grenades, and Messerchmidt fighter planes being shot down by American pilots; war to a six year old German child meant hiding in cellars, shuddering at the sound of air-raid sirens, and not having enough to eat. All of this eventually being followed by the occupation of brutal Russian troops. I had never seen a war movie like my American counterparts and was totally engulfed in fear at this point because all of the adults surrounding me were so afraid.

The summary of this catastrophic debacle, called World War II, can most easily be stated in terms of lost human lives, both military and civilian. The heaviest casualty fell to the USSR, losing 20 million military and civilian lives. In total, however, 55 million deaths resulted from this war, 30 million of them civilians.

This, by the way, does not include the 6 million Jews exterminated in the Holocaust. Now, considering the fact that 36 million innocent civilians died violently during this period, ask yourself how many of those were Americans. The answer of course is virtually none. This will give you some idea as to the difference in the way that we Europeans view war as opposed to those living in America.

My Escape from East Germany

My Escape from East Germany

CHAPTER VII
The Ami Conquerors

The next few years of our lives is a mixture of those incidents which I personally recall and those that have been passed on to me through my mother, Rosel, and Erich. Having heard most of these experiences so frequently, it sometimes becomes blurred as to that which I remember and that which has been passed on.

After emerging from the cellar we stood helplessly like lost souls on the cobblestone street. An American soldier wanted to know who lived in the house. Very timidly my mother raised her hand and accepted responsibility of ownership, although our housekeepers, a middle-aged couple by the name of Lebows, inhabited the first floor, and another couple, the Feurstags, rented the top floor from our family. The soldiers insisted that we all follow them through the front door while they conducted an inspection, most likely looking for any German soldiers that may have been hiding inside.

This happens to be one of my very clear recollections. They searched the living room from top to bottom coming across a large wooden box, which my Uncle Guenther, the Nazi, had sent from Berlin for storage near the war's end. They asked my mom about the contents of the box, to which she replied that it contained only harmless books. With that, the soldier pried it open with his bayonet, to find directly on top a copy of *Mein Kampf*. I remember the gasp that escaped from my mother's mouth, as hard as she tried to hold it back. Apparently the Americans, or at least some of them, were aware of the inflammatory writings of the Führer, and the frenetic soldier threw the book across the room as hard as he could. Things went downhill from there.

The two soldiers insisted that we accompany them in their room to room search, as they walked to my father's library and sitting room. They were quite intrigued by all of his camera equipment, as he loved his hobby of photography and possessed all of the latest Leica cameras and movie equipment. Then one of the Americans noticed my father's Iron Cross medal on a nearby shelf, which he had earned for bravery. What followed was not a pleasant happening for a young girl such as myself. The soldier, in a rage of fury that was initiated with the finding of *Mein Kampf*, took the Iron Cross like a Frisbee and hurled it towards the window. Unfortunately, his aim was poor and its sharp edge caught me in the leg. The medal imbedded into my thigh. I remember the angry look on his face when he threw the medal, and how quickly it changed to regret after he saw where it landed. I guess one could make excuses for him understanding that he had spent the past several months in mortal combat against our fellow countrymen. In addition to the fact that, as I later discovered, he was Jewish and had witnessed many of the horrors of the liberated concentration camps. Obviously finding both the book and the medal created quite an impulsive stir within him, and he simply lost control of his emotions.

On the brighter side, the Americans at least had the decency to quickly send for a medic, who gave me some sort of leather to chew on, while he sewed up my leg with no anesthesia. I still remember how sorry they were; however, it didn't prevent them from taking my father's entire collection of expensive camera equipment. I suppose it's true: "to the victors go the spoils."

I'll never forget how meticulously the Americans searched every corner in every room, most likely looking for mementos of their victory. Fortunately, our secret hiding place beneath the stairwell, where Erich used to conceal himself before scaring me still remained undiscovered.

This insignificant location held many of my father's photo albums that were still in place when I returned nineteen years later in 1964 to visit my mother, Rosel, and Erich, then living in Berlin. During that visit I made a side trip to Quedlinburg to visit my home on Breite Strasse and just for fun crept into Erich's hiding place to retrieve the photographs my father had so carefully taken during his tour of military duty in France, Belgium, and Russia.

About an hour after the American soldiers had left the house, there was a knock on the door, and to our great surprise, one of them had returned with two friends; arms loaded with all sorts of packages. Interestingly enough, when they were searching the house earlier, my mother and Rosel, now an attractive 21-year-old *frauline*, were petrified of being there alone with them with no men around to protect them. Lebows and Feuerstags were nowhere to be found. They had simply disappeared into the woodwork. When they looked out of their windows and saw the soldiers returning with all sorts of packages, they suddenly reappeared as if from thin air.

Everyone congregated in the living room as the Americans dumped boxes of chocolate, chewing gum, coffee, and C-rations on the floor with cardboard containers of powdered milk and two bottles of wine. As you might imagine, our renters, the Feuerstgs, and housekeepers, the Lebows, were the first to grab for the goodies. The soldier, who had thrown the Iron Cross, immediately withdrew his pistol and yelled "*Halt.*" That ended the grab-fest as they were told to leave *"schnell."* The Amis had apparently picked up some German vocabulary.

I had never tasted American chocolate or chewing gum and proceeded to treat this as a feast. Toward the end of the war food was getting scarce for the German civilians, as everything went to the soldiers at the front. We basically lived off of produce grown by a farmer who leased land from my parents outside the city. Occasionally he provided us with pork or chicken or even a rabbit, but more often than not, my mother concocted something edible from a lard type mixture. We called it "grease brei", supposedly very nutritious.

By 1945 I had celebrated my seventh birthday, with father still being held in an English prison camp somewhere in Europe. Our small family fended for ourselves during this American occupation.

Next to our home was an abandoned Jewish synagogue where I used to play, without even knowing the building's significance. Adjacent to the synagogue a school housed many of the occupying soldiers. One morning we were roused by a knock on the door and outside stood two American soldiers, but the only things I recall seeing were the rifles they carried. Still in shock from the Iron Cross incident, panic seized my entire body at the sight of uniforms and guns. Mother and Rosel followed me to the door, and I recall hiding behind Mom's skirt, absolutely petrified. The soldiers introduced themselves as Eddy and Lesty, and with Erich's limited English vocabulary, we determined that they wanted to use our home to do their daily clothes washing and bathing in return for bringing us coffee and candy. I'm not sure whether or not my mother had the option of refusing their offer but, needless to say, she accepted.

Thus started a rather friendly relationship with our enemy. Each evening Eddy and Lesty arrived at the house bringing coffee, candy, and chewing gum, setting their rifles carefully in the corner by their knapsacks. They washed their clothes, bathed, shaved, and Eddy always sang me a lullaby before putting me to bed. I really became very friendly with Eddy in only a way that a seven-year-old child can, and I still have fond memories of him to this day.

Eventually, the Americans were ordered to round up all German males living in the city in an effort to determine which ones were ex-soldiers or possibly soldiers in hiding. They discovered my gentle artist brother, Erich, who lasted only a few weeks in the German army before the officers realized his lack of suitability for military duties. At one point, while assigned to guard French prisoners, and being a devotee of French art, literature, and the French people, he self-destructed his military career. He sneaked food to them in return for their letting him sleep on duty, with the promise that they awaken him when German officers approached. In due time he was caught and discharged.

Being a true artist, Erich has spent his entire life painting his visions of Mozart's music and Shakespeare's plays while preaching pacifism. He studied art in night school in Quedlinburg and eventually at the Art Institute in Dresden. He hated everything the Nazis stood for, and spoke out frequently against Hitler, creating real angst among the adult members of our family and relatives.

Erich proved to be the most stabilizing influence upon my life. His love and appreciation of the arts compelled me to study hard in school and listen to classical music in my spare time. While attending art school in Quedlinburg, and working part time for a gardening firm, the state saw fit to draft him into the Hitler Youth, which he despised. Given no alternative, he later became a private in the army. My mother strutted like a proud peacock walking down the street with Erich when he was in uniform. He so resented the Heil Hitler salute, however, that he intentionally riveted his attention to shop windows or looked away when a German army officer approached, in order to avoid performing this obscene gesture.

So Erich's brief military service qualified him to be held in the American prison camp several miles from our home. It took only a short time before the Americans realized that Erich could never have been a serious threat as a soldier, so they provided him the papers indicating his release. This actually disappointed Erich as he later stated that he had never been fed so well and treated so decently. Upon release, he walked through the cold, muddy countryside eventually making his way back home. As he passed through some of the small villages the locals treated him quite shabbily. Why should he be walking free when their own sons or husbands remained in American prison camps?

Erich, a virtual invalid today, is now 79 years old living in a nursing home in Berlin with crippling Rheumatoid arthritis, developed when he was in his late forties. His entire life has been devoted to painting and the love of art. He has never married, and in a sense has now become my ward. Today, as he views documentaries on television relating to the Nazi atrocities, he still becomes violent with rage and indignation that his countrymen could be so cruel.

CHAPTER VIII

My Promiscuous Parents

Earlier I referred to philandering parents and, in an effort to be forthright, I want to provide a painful but factual accounting. During the war my sister Rosel, at the age of 19, worked as an apprentice learning to become a secretary. She became engaged to a handsome young man by the name of Harry Krause, who also worked in Quedlinburg. According to my sister, who later related this story to me, Harry frequently found time to visit my mom while Rosel worked. Rosel had often wondered why her mother so encouraged this relationship, but she simply dismissed it as a whim of the usual mother that doesn't want to see her daughter grow up to be a spinster. It hadn't occurred to her that with my father being away in the war my mom had become very lonely.

One night Harry, Rosel, and my mom sat around the living room drinking so heavily that Harry couldn't find his way to the front door. In the course of the evening they had all apparently fallen asleep, when in fact, none of them had. Thinking that Rosel was a very heavy sleeper, her fiancée and my mother proceeded to make love. This devastated Rosel, as she pretended to sleep. Having discovered that this was not the first such incident between the two, Rosel threw him out in the street. Harry, subsequently drafted into the army, went to the Russian front and never returned. The relationship that followed between my mother and Rosel never quite recovered; however, they did manage to live together for the next 30 years.

At the same time, loneliness also overtook my father, while off fighting Hitler's wars. The custom of housing German officers in private homes in cities where their troops were stationed proved to be too great a temptation. In 1940, after returning from the campaign in France, he was stationed in Duesberg in northern Germany and housed by a wealthy couple who owned a shipping company. It seems that the husband spent too much time looking after his freighters while his wife, Sophie Gussman, waltzed around the house in see-through negligees to taunt my father. The result of all of this was a torrid affair between my father and Mrs. Gussman, who later bought a summer home in the Harz Mountains, not far from Quedlinberg, just to be near my father. A more serious consequence resulted in the birth of my half-sister, Erica, named after my father, now living somewhere in Europe. I actually recall meeting Sophie Gussman when she dropped over for tea one day to visit my parents. My father had very good taste, as she was quite an attractive woman.

I can't help but feel that the climate of war and the loneliness of separation caused my parents' infidelities. Unfortunately, my mother's promiscuity displayed itself well after the war's end and after my father's death. My own boyfriend, as opposed to Rosel's, later became the object of her romantic exploits, but that's getting a little ahead of where I'm going for now.

CHAPTER IX
The Barbaric Intrusion

I never truly understood the logic behind Russian troops taking over our domain when it was the American soldiers who initially came to our city and "captured" us. How could we be treated so humanely by our first conquerors, and so brutally by the Russians that followed?

The answer, of course, lies in the politics of the agreements drawn up in Yalta, a city on the island of Crimea in Ukraine. In February, 1945, President Roosevelt of the United States, Winston Churchill of Great Britain, and Joseph Stalin of the USSR met to determine both a political and military strategy to deal with a crumbling Germany upon its defeat. As an afterthought they invited France to participate. The intention of the Yalta Conference involved the design of a plan that would "destroy German militarism and Nazism and ensure that Germany could never again be capable of disturbing the peace of the world." It also demanded that German war criminals be brought to justice.

The agreement divided Poland with the eastern portion absorbed by Russia while western Poland could expand at the expense of German territory. One of the confidential agreements at Yalta stated that Russia promised to declare war on Japan within ninety days of Germany's surrender in return for additional territories in Asia. Stalin had made a shrewd agreement, since Russia's declaration of war on Japan came after the United States had nuked them into submission in August of 1945 by dropping atomic bombs on Hiroshima and Nagasaki.

In August of 1945, President Truman, who succeeded FDR upon his death, met with Stalin and Churchill in Potsdam and implemented the Yalta Agreement. In addition to outlawing the Nazi party and taking steps to make certain that Germany would never again become a military power, the Potsdam agreement divided Germany into four zones controlled by the United States, Great Britain, France, and the

USSR. This agreement's significance to my family and me was earth-shaking. The division dramatically devastated our lives and put our peaceful, quaint, historic city of Quedlinburg in the Russian barbarians' cruel grasp. I cried as Eddy and Lesty abandoned us not realizing just how miserable life could be while in the hands of our new masters. Winston Churchill quite prophetically stated at the time in that an "Iron Curtain" had descended upon all of Eastern Europe. Quedlinburg fell on the wrong side of that curtain.

The next twelve years between the beginning of the Russian occupation and my eventual escape presented challenges that no teenager should face. Granted, I didn't remember much of the war itself, but the cultural shock during that period for those that influenced my life was traumatic.

The adults around me had lived through the "war to end all wars" between 1914 and 1918, an economy in the 20's that had gone completely out of control, and a reign of terror under the most violent mad man who had ever walked the face of the earth. Following World War II these adults faced the realities of the atrocities committed in their name. Now, under the rule of the Communists, their bitterest enemies, they were expected to conduct their lives, and influence the lives of the children of Nazi Germany.

I had now become aware of what surrounded me, and events began to etch their way into my long-term memory. No longer required to be dependent on my adult family to refresh my memories and thoughts regarding those events that directly affected my life, what follows is no longer hearsay.

Gone were the friendly faces of Eddy and Lesty replaced by what appeared to be some sort of Asiatic looking creatures, most likely the Mongolian troops assigned to the Russian army. Only a matter of days afterward a curfew descended upon the citizens of Quedlinburg, and all inhabitants were required to be in their homes by eight o'clock every night—something unique that the Americans never required during their short occupation. The impact of this curfew became very clear to me when I looked out of the window one night shortly before the magic hour and witnessed a scene that to this day haunts every bone in my body.

As described earlier, our house faced the intersection of Breite Strasse and Schulstrasse with the schoolyard adjacent to the neighboring synagogue visible from a window on our second floor. Following the customary pastime in Germany and many other parts of Europe, I happened to be looking out that window one evening just as the curfew deadline approached. I spotted two girls in their late teens scurrying across the schoolyard heading home when eight or ten Russian soldiers roaming the streets looking for curfew violators caught sight of them. The two never made it home. As the soldiers approached the girls, I wanted to yell for them to come to our house as instinctively I felt the approaching danger. The words never came out of my mouth as the soldiers grabbed them and proceeded to take turns violently raping each of them, then passing their limp bodies to the next barbarian. When they finished using their two victims, I gagged as I witnessed them, right below my window, take their bayonets, place them on their rifles, and alternately plunge them into their bodies as if they were stuffed dummies used for bayonet practice. The bodies remained in the street until the next day when their parents were permitted to claim them.

Upon hearing the commotion my mother quickly made her way to the window to see me frozen in a state of both shock and panic unable to emit a sound. With my mouth wide open attempting to scream but nothing a stammer came forth as she tried to pull me away from the appalling scene. Like being chased by a monster in a dream but unable to call for help. In my state of trauma, I couldn't be budged as I gripped the windowsill with more strength than I actually possessed. Other soldiers had heard my mother's and sister's screams as they came to my side. They called for a Russian medic who paid us a visit some hours later to offer me a sedative. A lot of good that did!

For several months these Asiatic barbarians occasionally came to our house demanding that they be allowed to use the facilities. Each time I ran for cover under the nearest bed. It took quite some time before I ever got a decent night's sleep, and the dreams that followed, when I did sleep, presented the same harrowing nightmare. This incident took place over 56 years ago, and to this day I will not permit myself to witness a movie scene where some woman is overpowered by a male perpetrator. Even the hint of a rape scene to come drives me out of the theater in anticipation of it. I had been introduced to our new masters, the soldiers of Communist Russia.

When I say that our home became an "on demand" facility for the Russians, I presume that most other homes in the city received the same treatment. The next incident took place few days after the rape when two soldiers had found some berries in a nearby field. They stopped at our house to wash off the dirt and the first receptacle they spotted containing water was the toilet. While one of them proceeded to rinse the fruit, the other played with the pull-chain that flushes the toilet. It was clear to my mother that these animals had used the woods their entire lives as their waste dumps, and had never seen indoor plumbing with flush toilets. With one pull the berries disappeared in a whirlpool, and the two men were beside themselves with anger and frustration. Being uncivilized savages, both of them began to demolish the toilet.

Eventually word got out that my mother excelled as a seamstress. One of the soldiers, while intruding in our home, had watched her sewing a dress for me out of some old material. Since there were so many promotions handed out rewarding their victory over the German army, many insignias had to be applied to the uniforms. Unfortunately, no official insignias were available, so they pressed my mother into duty forcing her to sew makeshift insignias and applying them to the uniforms.

At one point two of the female officers requested that my mother sew dresses for them and ordered her to deliver the finished garments to the barracks. They provided her with a special pass to access the street where they lived. As she approached the barracks that evening to make her delivery, she noticed that they were all in the midst of a party flowing with liquor. They invited her in and insisted that she drink her share of vodka before providing her payment for the dresses. After a few hours they took the suitcase my mother used to carry the dresses and filled it with flour, sugar, rice, bread, and what appeared to be lard. This concoction served as payment for the dresses. The suitcase was so heavy when filled that one of the soldiers carried it home for her. After arriving home she opened the suitcase and dumped the contents on the kitchen table. They hadn't bothered to wrap any of the commodities separately so this unappetizing conglomeration of starch provided us with meals for the next several days.

In due time soldiers from central Russia replaced the invading Asiatics as the complaints of rapes, murders, and vandalism continued to mount. Also, as a result of this uninhibited behavior, the army moved to Kasernes outside the city. The enlisted men were required to be in squad size groups accompanied by an officer before being permitted to reenter the city limits. It seemed that by my eighth or ninth birthday things had actually become somewhat more stable and even bearable.

My Escape from East Germany

CHAPTER X
Stasi—The Police from Hell

Transition may be a way of life for most; but when I think about the developments imposed upon our sixteen million inhabitants of what officially became the German Democratic Republic, East Germany, the changes were startlingly abrupt. If two world wars, total economic disintegration, and life under a fascist regime were not sufficient, the transition from Nazism to Communism shattered the strongest of constitutions, my family's included.

Not to dwell upon history, but to understand the underlying intention that created the need for this story to be told, it is necessary to comprehend the conditions that incited its creation.

In 1949, after my eleventh birthday, the Soviet Union established the Communist dictatorship governing East Germany. They installed Walter Ulbricht, with dictatorial authority over our new country, and charged him with the responsibility to transform the German Democratic Republic into a major Communist power. He ruled with an iron discipline often compared to that of the Soviet leader Joseph Stalin. Imagine the common German citizen living one day under the right wing dictatorship of a Hitler, and the next day the left wing tyranny of an Ulbricht. Confusing to say the least.

The Communist Party completely controlled the government, which in turn had taken over all industry, large and small, as well as agriculture. Both heavy industry and farm production primarily focused on satisfying the needs of the Soviet Union. In fact, as difficult times encompassed Russia, production quotas were dramatically increased in the factories and on the farms. The workers, unable to keep up with the new measures, revolted in 1953, but Soviet troops were brought in to suppress the uprising in their typically violent manner.

Life became so intolerable for many of the industrious and talented in East Germany, that many fled to the west where the American and British established controls in accordance with the Potsdam Agreement. Unwilling to lose this cadre of skilled personnel, Ulbricht established a corridor of armed police along the border dividing East and West Germany, thus converting our country into a prison with no escape. The final barrier, or keystone, to this barricade was established in 1961, shortly after my own escape, with the construction of the infamous Berlin Wall.

It is of interest to note that, while most citizens possessed an overwhelming desire to get out, others, such as my brother Erich, regret, even to this day, the fact that they ever left the confines and "comforts" of Communist rule. Always the consummate artist content to live off of the crumbs thrown to him by the government, while devoting himself to his paintings. As brilliant as he is, he will forgive neither my mother nor me for dragging him across the border to freedom.

To comprehend life in the German Democratic Republic means understanding East Germany's Ministry for State Security, commonly referred to as the Stasi. The Stasi, established in 1950 provided an all-encompassing web of informants to repress the citizens of East Germany.

Just to illustrate the pervasiveness of this ruthless and formidable organization of secret police, it must be compared in breadth to its previously existing counterparts equally capable of instilling terror. The notorious KGB in Russia, many of whom were actually appalled at the methods employed by the Stasi, enlisted nearly 500,000 full-time agents, or one for every 5800 citizens. The Gestapo in Nazi Germany engaged one agent for every 2000 citizens. The Stasi recruited 175,000 official informants including nearly 100,000 uniformed agents to spy on their citizenry of 16 million people, *or one agent for every 90 people*. Try imagining living your daily life knowing that one out of every 90 people you know, or come in contact with, are being paid to inform an oppressive government about your daily activities. Not only your actions but also your every day conversations. The worst part being that I never knew which one of the ninety were informers. Believe it or not, family members often spied on each other for fear of threats, blackmail, or even in return for monetary rewards. To this day, I look back on some of my closest friends, with whom I'm still in contact, and have doubts about their loyalties during that period.

When returning to my home in Quedlinburg in 1968, eight years after I had immigrated to the United States, I decided to pay a surprise visit to Bimbo, my closest friend during my teenage years. I had been visiting my family in Berlin, and decided to take the three hour train ride to Quedlinburg, the city I still call home. I thought it would be fun to visit with some of my old school cronies and playmates.

Bimbo and I had long ago perfected a whistle signal to get the other's attention. I walked to Bimbo's apartment house and stood on the street whistling and calling Bimbo's name. She still lived on the fourth floor of the same building. Having not seen each other in over ten years, I thought I would see her drapes open widely and the window lifted briskly, in her excitement to see me. To my great disappointment, once she caught sight of me she waved me away with her one hand while motioning with the other that her walls had ears. My family, still listed in the Stasi black book because of our escape from East Germany, might create serious problems for anyone seen talking to me. I understood her dilemma. To this day I'm not certain whether or not she may have been one of the paid informers.

On the other hand, there was Achim, one of my dearest friends upon whom I could always depend. Achim and his wife, Ilsa, owned a bus company in Quedlinburg that the government permitted him to operate under the Stasi's closest scrutiny. As one of the few entrepreneurs, and therefore someone for whom the Stasi had no use, and even less trust, he lived under a police microscope. In his living room sat a television set for which he had waited three years. Achim informed me that all of our conversations were to take place outside of that room, as a listening device had been implanted during its construction. The government controlled the electronics industry making it quite easy for them implant such devices, particularly on products ordered three years in advance. Actually that lead-time seemed short in comparison to the seven years it took to get a car delivered. He couldn't remove the device without the Stasi's knowledge.

Achim further informed me that they had tapped his phone and frequently opened his mail before it arrived at his house. He could also encounter considerable harassment for hosting me as an afternoon visitor for the same reason that Bimbo refused to see me. Fortunately, Achim, a truly independent soul, gladly welcomed me to spend the day with his family; Stasi be damned.

Although my hosts during that return visit, the Lebows, informed me that I must register with them by signing a book and leaving my passport, I had forgotten. When I returned to their home four police cars waited for me at the front door. Little did I realize the seriousness of my forgetfulness. From that point forward plain clothes Stasi followed me day and night wherever I went during my short stay in Quedlinburg. Although this feeling of being followed seemed eerie at first, it became almost comical by the second day. In one restaurant I even asked the waitress to bring them a glass of wine with my compliments as they sat behind their newspapers observing me from a distant table.

The Stasi's methods were ruthless and efficient in squelching dissent—totally unrestrained. I have since discovered that they maintained files on six million citizens, more than one third of the entire population of East Germany. They routinely tapped telephones, monitored mail, and infiltrated every social club, youth organization, and factory. They even went to the trouble of gathering the scents of thousands of suspected dissidents by wiping their clothes on objects they had touched and storing them in sealed containers in the event the need ever arose to release bloodhounds in search of them. Hundreds of thousands of innocents were imprisoned, including my own mother, under intolerable conditions, with torture a way of life in extracting information.

You can now understand the environment under which we were forced to live until 1957, by which time I found it no longer bearable. Circumstances then compelled Mommy and I to seek another way of life and prompted our escape to the West that I will later describe in detail. Little wonder why East German citizens daily sacrificed their lives by the hundreds attempting to escape across the border to freedom: a border lined with watchtowers every few hundred meters and manned with snipers to execute those trying to sneak across. Between the Russians and the Stasi, they had converted an entire country into a prison.

CHAPTER XI
Survival Continues—Olympic Training

Being the local "tomboy," at the tender age of twelve, I attended school each day leaving the house dressed with the finest clothes my mother could tailor and returning each day covered with mud, scratches, and torn clothes. I couldn't resist climbing every tree in the neighborhood and scrounging through basements of war torn buildings. My teachers, however, considered me a decent student but somewhat of a disciplinary problem.

Athletics truly attracted my attention. Even at the age of nine I competed favorably with boys when it came to track and field events, and actually surpassed many of them. Although I looked upon such events as frivolous sport, I wasn't aware until much later that the enormous shadow of the Communist bureaucracy viewed these activities in a far more serious light.

Germans had always placed an abnormally high level of importance on athletics and used it as a showcase for the world to see the superiority of the German culture as evidenced by the 1938 Olympics held in Berlin. This event, Hitler's anticipated moment of triumph, ended in his total frustration as a black American, Jesse Owens, decimated the German runners. His rage intensified by the fact that not only had an American run off with the honors but a "black" American. Hitler hated the blacks almost as much as he despised the Jews.

Once the Communists ruled the East, they too chose the Olympics as their showcase. To the Russians, however, athletics became more of a religion than athletic competition for sport. They scouted the country's youth at the kindergarten level and nurtured and trained them until they were either cast aside or earmarked to prepare for the Olympics. You only have to look at the number of medals won by East Germany relative to their tiny population in comparison to the United States and the rest of the world. On a per capita basis, they dominated the Olympic Games for over twenty years.

It therefore became incumbent upon me as one who simply enjoyed sports as early as my eighth birthday, to uphold the dignity of the East German masters. As a result, I found myself in a school where four hours of every day were devoted to participating in various athletic activities. I actually found this to be great fun, since homework was de-emphasized and the stress on academic work virtually non-existent. Coaches and teachers watched very closely as we unknowingly, at first, were going through a selection process. This went on for about six to nine months until my ninth birthday when they placed me in a special school that concentrated even more heavily on athletics and less on my studies. The school enrolled about 120 students between the ages of eight and sixteen, and the selection process became even more intense.

What more could I have asked for? Doing what I enjoyed without having the pressure of having to study and do homework. Not until much later in my life did I become aware of how seriously this process diluted my entire youth. Instead of training my mind to cope with life's future challenges, the "State" trained my body to compete in meaningless events to enhance the "glory" of the German Democratic Republic.

The new school, located in Quedlinburg, continued the cutting and selection process, but now we actively competed against students who had been relocated from other cities to attend the school. We all lived in dilapidated dormitories; however, living nearby, I received permission to go home on the weekends. Apparently my athletic skills met with the observing coaches' approval as I continually made the cut. Informally they made me the co-ed soccer team's captain. In fact, I seemed to be a natural leader when it came to other extracurricular activities such as climbing trees to steal pears in the local orchard, or stealing eggs from the nearby chicken coops to help provide food for the family.

I feel hesitant to admit that that I stole property let alone boast about the fact that I was a thief. We lived under the Communist regime, which supposedly provided equal shares for everyone. "No one goes hungry." On the contrary, it seemed that everyone suffered from hunger. There just wasn't enough food available. One means of support for those my age involved collecting Japanese Beetles from our local farmers' potato plants. Imagine the misery of crawling around in the mud during cold wet weather picking these ugly creatures from the potato leaves and putting them in glass jars. Our meager reward consisted of two pounds of flour for each jar we filled. It took me one entire weekend day to fill a jar but this tedious task virtually helped sustain our family. Mommy had devised many different recipes that that utilized the flour along with several other unknown ingredients to feed us. As time progressed, collecting beetles was an expected duty that my mother imposed upon me, as Rosel's pride wouldn't let her stoop that low, and Erich's laziness claimed that a task not related to arts wasted his time.

By my eleventh birthday, my coaches and teachers declared me to be considerably undernourished, and sent me to a sanatorium in the mountains 40 kilometers from Quedlinburg to be "fattened up." By feeding me special foods and forcing me to take naps outside on the deck overlooking the mountains, they intended to increase my energy level. They really only managed to increase my level of desire to stay there as long as I could, so I could eat well and sleep as much as much as I pleased. Sitting outside on the sunny patio overlooking the scenery that only the lovely Harz Mountains could render brought a degree of serenity far beyond anything that I might have dreamed about in this world of wars and tyranny. More importantly, I had no classes with which to contend, and actually had become somewhat bored by all of the athletics back in the school environment. I enjoyed the sanatorium so much that I convinced them that I needed an additional four weeks beyond the prescribed time period.

CHAPTER XII
Father Returns From the War

Meanwhile, as sports and school continued to occupy my daily activities, my family became more and more concerned about my father's return from the British prison camp. In 1948, and after an unreasonably lengthy detention, Pappi, as I often called him, came home a changed man. Although I never really got that close to him earlier because of our rather significant age gap, as well as the amount of time he spent away from home, it seemed as though now I didn't know him at all. In 1944 at the age of six I'd last seen him. It had been four years since our family was together, and it required the start of an entire reacquainting process involving my father and myself.

Between Mommy, Erich, and Rosel there seemed to be a contrived attitude of enthusiasm for the purpose of building up my anticipation for his return. I became weary of hearing the artificial excitement in their voices when every other word from one of the three of them was "Pappi's coming home, Pappi's coming home," in an effort to arouse my own excitement, as though it would be contagious. There may have been sincerity on my mother's part, but Rosel and Erich's voices didn't seem that genuine. The warrior had returned, but the circumstances were not terribly conducive to a cheerful celebration.

The East German government, a Communist system against which he bitterly fought for the past five years, had usurped his steel fabricating company. Grudgingly he returned to work in his own company as an office employee and manager under the close scrutiny of a Communist Party delegate. His experiences during the war were something of which he rarely ever spoke, and the time in the prison camp was not even mentioned. Of course, at the age of ten, what did I know of prison camps? My father returned as a very proud but very sad individual. His despondency put a further damper on an already depressing situation for the family.

CHAPTER XIII
Rosel Goes to Prison

The love between sisters can truly be overwhelming. Rosel and I treasure such a relationship. Being fourteen years older than I, she had become my mentor, guardian, confidante, and dearest friend in addition to being my older sister.

As I write this today, Rosel, at the age of 78, sits in a nursing home in Berlin with an oppressive case of Alzheimer's disease. She is alone, totally unaware of her surroundings. Before visiting her in Berlin just recently I stopped at a small gift shop next to the nursing home to buy her a modest present: a child's zipper purse in the shape of a small furry dog. Rosel had owned a long hair Dachshund for many years that she dearly loved and which had become part of our family until its untimely death. I thought that this token would remind her of Feline.

As I entered her room and first saw her sitting by the window staring off into a never-never land, my stomach literally turned sour. I thought the nurse had given me the wrong room number as I looked at a woman who had aged twenty years during the past twelve months. She gave me a slight hint of recognition as if to acknowledge a cleaning woman that had come to mop the floors. My eyes filled with tears as I watched my sister stare at me with her tongue dangling from the side of her mouth not even aware of my presence.

I handed her the purse that she gratefully accepted as a faint smile of gratitude surfaced on her face. I spoke in soft loving tones while she alternated her attention between the furry purse and me. Rosel gave no response to my conversation and most likely didn't even know me. I couldn't hold back the tears any longer as it seemed so incomprehensible that my sister and closest ally of sixty-three years felt more comfortable petting her new toy than acknowledging my presence after not having seen each other for two years. I felt that my presence was meaningless to Rosel but knew that I must stay long enough to at least provide the opportunity to arouse some of her emotions. No such luck. After a heart-rending hour I left in a state of despair and hollow depression. In a sense, her separation from reality probably serves her well and has become a blessing. I would at least like to believe that to be true.

This woman, when I was 10 years old and greatly undernourished, illegally sneaked across the border, not far from our city, to get the desperately needed cod liver oil that the doctors had recommended for my diet. East Germans frequently smuggled wares such as wine into the West in exchange for cigarettes, medicine, food, and cod liver oil, goods that were unobtainable to those of us in the East. Yes, wine from the Harz Mountains had actually become a sought after commodity in the West, even to those who had access to the wonderful vineyards along the Rhine River. Not only was Harz wine savory, but also quite inexpensive. Getting to the border crossing became a somewhat complicated process as it involved taking a train to one of the border towns and walking through the woods across the boundary at night. The infamous watchtowers later manned by snipers with floodlights had not yet been erected. That came a few years later.

Rosel knew that she willingly exposed herself to a dangerous situation and if caught could suffer severe consequences. Every now and then Erich accompanied her on these missions; however, he tired easily and declined after the first two or three. Rosel, a very pretty woman at the age of 24, brought out the envy in some of her acquaintances. This petty jealousy, or possibly the thought of a reward, prompted someone to inform the Russian authorities concerning her exploits. The penalty she suffered changed the life of our entire family.

It started with a knock on our door one night in the summer of 1948 after we had all gone to bed. My father had just recently returned. Uncle Guenther had departed for Bavaria, Erich labored in a floral research station, and Rosel worked as an executive secretary for a local manufacturer. Mommy spent much of her time as a seamstress for the Russian army, as well as the locals, and things were getting back to a more normalized condition.

Late night disturbances were not unusual during that period, but when the door opened, and three Russian KGB agents marched in, a penetrating chill of fear overwhelmed me. They unceremoniously grabbed my sister, handcuffed her, and formally stated that she was under arrest. Without so much as a brief explanation, they marched her to the waiting vehicle and drove to Halle where they interrogated her that night in the local prison.

I remember standing in the living room, mouth wide open, unable to utter a sound. I felt as though these monsters had been transported from my recent nightmares to reality. They actually stomped into our home, grabbed my sister, and marched her to a waiting truck as though she were a viscous criminal. I stared at my mother who stood motionless with a look of resignation on her face that said, "it was only a matter of time before Rosel got caught." Caught at what? Helping her younger sister to survive? That's a crime? I shuddered with fright and cried. At that point my fear had turned to anger and hate as I felt the unfairness of our plight living under these Russian brutes. At the age of ten I had determined first that I would do anything possible to help my sister, and secondly, I would not spend the remainder of my life in these prison-like surroundings.

Two days after these animals had so crudely marched Rosel out of our home, we again heard the familiar sound of a jeep pulling up to the house and the loud knock of the KGB on our front door. It's a knock like no other knock. Like a hammer driving a nail through heavy oak with the malicious intent of intimidating anyone within earshot. It's a knock that freezes your insides before you are overcome with a sick feeling of revulsion. I simply stood in our living room frozen to the floor. Not again?

Yes, again. We hadn't yet recovered from Rosel's abduction when the same three agents walked in demanding that the family assemble in the living room. This action typified the harassment so often employed by the Russian oppressors. They not only attacked the accused, but took relish in emotionally abusing their family and relatives. Without any hesitation, the one in command abruptly demanded that we remain where we were in the living room while they conducted an unobstructed search of the entire house starting with the third floor bedrooms looking for Rosel's contraband goods.

The living room in our house blended into the dining area with a small partition dividing the two. Against the far wall of the dining room stood a large wooden chest of drawers that extended from floor to ceiling where my mother stored her finest china. A small gap of about three inches separated the bottom of the chest from the floor. The chest's lower section jutted out from the top section causing my mother considerable grief when I climbed up on it to get access to the top drawers. Rosel had once told me in confidence that she had concealed her goodies in the top drawer of the dining room chest.

As the Stasi initiated the upstairs search, they departed from the living room leaving us alone. Still feeling the pain of Rosel's seizure, and without giving a great deal of thought to the consequences, I ran to the dining room chest, jumped on the lower section and opened the top drawer nearest the ceiling. In a state of both panic and exhilaration I grabbed the cigarette cartons, chocolates, a few packages of silk stockings, jumped back to the floor and stuffed the entire batch under the chest as far back as I could reach. Unknown to my parents, I often used this space as my own personal hiding place for things I hid from both them and Erich.

My motive, of course, reflected a deep love for Rosel, as I thought that if nothing out of the ordinary were found, they would release her much sooner. Not only wasn't this the case, but in reflecting back, it was apparent that they simply wanted the goods for themselves. Following the bedroom search, they started in the living room, and the first place they looked was in the ceiling cabinet where the goods were originally hidden. The four of us were stricken with an almost electrifying tenseness as they continued hunting, and we felt a great triumph when they admitted being denied the victory of finding the smuggled merchandise. Their frustration was obvious as they departed, but they left us with the clear indication that they would be back. They did return for the next three nights and never once found my secret hiding place.

I'll never forget my father, after their first search and departure, how he realized what I had done, and came over to hug me as he had never done before. He was far from being a warm individual, but that night his emotions were not to be denied.

Years later Rosel related to me the terrifying and tragic experiences she was forced to endure during her captivity. Although overwhelmed by the humiliation, she still insisted on telling us in detail how the workings of the Russian mind could be so deceptive that a rational person would never understand their logic.

Although my beloved sister admitted to the "crime" of bartering wine for cod liver oil, the Russians attempted to force her to admit to a totally different offense—that she had been spying for the West. How ludicrous, yet how tragic.

The Russians had set up a temporary jail in Halle that they used as a holding tank to break down suspects before hauling them off to the larger prison camps from where many inmates never returned. The building, a crude brick unheated structure, consisted of eight cells separated by cinder block walls with makeshift barred doors on each cell locked with a heavy chain. In one corner of the building stood a room with concrete walls and a solid metal door not visible from the other cells. This enclosure was used primarily for those unwilling to readily admit to crimes that they had not committed—the notorious water torture chamber.

Rosel told us of her treatment in the Halle prison where they had held her for one of the most terrifying weeks of her life, most of that time spent in the corner cell. It was late fall, the weather had turned cold, and they forced her to strip down to her bra and panties to stand in ankle deep cold water in the center of the room. She stood for hours at a time with cold droplets of water intermittently falling on her head from a faucet that had been installed in the ceiling. She tried to keep herself warm by wrapping her arms around her body as one does when they stand outside shivering in freezing weather, but there was no relief from the unfriendly cold that permeated her entire body. She attempted to predict when the next drop would fall; however, the pattern was so random that the anticipation alone drove her to mental distraction. The Russians had apparently adopted a version of the old Chinese water torture and were applying it to my unsuspecting sister.

They were clever enough to keep her just the right amount of time in the chamber to prevent her from passing out before returning her to her individual cell. That would have made it too easy on her, as they wanted Rosel to remain sufficiently awake and alert to experience the sheer agony of her torment. They wanted a confession to something for which she wasn't guilty, but she feared that falsely admitting to spying would result in even more torturous consequences. As a result, she admitted only to her clandestine border crossings, a fact with which the Russians didn't appear to be too concerned.

At night, these Russian masters of mental torture made certain that sleep would be an unattainable luxury. A guard stationed outside of Rosel's cell entered when her eyes closed and slapped her face with a ruler, not hard enough to leave bruises, but enough to make sure she stayed awake. Rosel reached the point that she would have admitted to anything including starting the Second World War if she thought her jailers would ease up on her.

As a last resort, they put another woman in Rosel's cell who told Rosel that the Russians had finally coerced her into admitting to being a spy. Rosel watched the royal treatment this woman received along with the extra food and bedding. Even though it was obvious to Rosel that this woman was indeed a "plant," Rosel told her that she was ready to sign any papers that they would place in front of her if that would bring an end to the torture. Word immediately got to the authorities that Rosel had broken and they instantly prepared the necessary papers for her to sign the following day.

That night they permitted Rosel to get a full night's sleep, but either fortunately or unfortunately, she had a powerful dream in which my mother adamantly told her not to confess to anything. I suppose that dreams affect each of us differently; however, in looking back at the outcome of that particular dream, it resulted in disaster for my sister. When they presented the papers to her for signature the next morning she refused to sign, thinking back on her dream. Without any hesitation the officer in charge sentenced her to three years in Sachsenhausen, a former Nazi concentration camp north of Berlin that the Russians had converted to a maximum security prison.

For me a nightmare had come true. No one could imagine how the news had so brutally crushed my insides. My mouth became parched and everything inside of me felt hollow when Pappi walked in the front door, sat Mommy and I in the living room, and began to relate the story of his visit earlier in the day to the Halle jail.

When he asked to see Rosel for a few moments, they briskly stated that she no longer had the "luxury" of staying in that prison. They further informed him that she was in transit to Sachsenhausen for an indefinite period of confinement and that he should resign himself to the fact that he may never see her again.

My sister, my closest friend, and soul mate had been abruptly removed from my life and now they were telling us that we may never again be graced by her presence. Tears wanted to invade my eyes but the shock and terror overwhelmed them as I sat speechless with my parents knowing that nothing could be done to change the outcome determined by these ruthless bastards.

Rosel continued her narrative by telling us about the conditions faced by a prisoner in a camp run by both East German and Russian police. The two apparently tried to outdo each other in their efforts to make life miserable for the inmates. The diet consisted of moldy dried bread and watered soup that smelled like three day old sewage. If she wanted to perform the luxury of washing her hair to rid herself of lice, they forced her to use her own urine. Rosel did have the good fortune of running into one of her old friends, another inmate who happened to be pregnant. This woman was allowed some extra kitchen privileges that permitted her to occasionally sneak some potatoes to Rosel helping to make life somewhat more bearable.

Although my sister was originally sentenced to three years, an amnesty was declared in 1950 for minor offense criminals, and Rosel was freed after serving only two years of the three year term. When my mother, who had been sick with worry ever since Rosel had been taken away, and father heard the news of the amnesty, they walked to the train station every day in the hope of greeting Rosel upon her return. Circumstances prevented her from coming home immediately, so my parents returned empty, dejected, and frustrated during that first week.

One day my mother's stomach cramps that had been causing her severe weight loss were getting the best of her. My father stayed home to care for her. That afternoon I wanted to stay close to home and spent my time playing my favorite game of solitaire in the front yard. This consisted of spinning a top on the sidewalk and hitting it with a stick to keep it turning. Out of nowhere I heard a soft voice behind me saying "Barbelshen, I'm home," and I knew instantly it was my sister. I couldn't remember a happier day in my life, and I jumped up and down and cried, I was so overjoyed. My big sister and closest friend had at last come home.

We later discovered the reason that Rosel had delayed her return to Quedlinburg was the result of meeting a gentleman by the name of Guenther Glorius during her tenure in Sachsenhausen. It didn't take a lot of encouragement for people to fall in love under the dire conditions of prison camp life, so when Rosel and Guenther were released at the same time, they decided to spend their first few days together in West Berlin. She came to see us following those few days, but only after promising Guenther that she would return to him in Berlin. This, of course, took place before the infamous Berlin Wall was erected, and people were permitted to take the U-Bahn and S-Bahn between East and West Berlin. Rosel did go back to Berlin to marry Guenther after spending only a few days with us, and I remember how the thought of losing her again devastated me. This time, however, I was comforted by the knowledge that it was only a temporary separation.

Guenther Glorious had been an officer in the Wehrmacht, the German army, and had come from a well-to-do family in Bochum, West Germany, prior to the war. The Russians had accused him of sabotage and had imprisoned him in Sachsenhausen at the end of the war. During his lengthy tenure there he had developed a severe case of open Tuberculosis, which eventually claimed his life four years following his release. Rosel also contracted the formidable disease during her prison stay, however, not quite to the degree of Guenther's case. They were two lonely souls travelling home on the bus, sharing a common misery, and married out of desperation.

I remember their returning shortly thereafter to Quedlinburg to be married by a local Justice of the Peace in order to please my parents. Guenther, a truly a pleasant man had a wonderful sense of humor. After spending a few days with him before they returned to Berlin as a married couple, I learned to really enjoy

Guenther and must admit that I was thrilled for my sister, even though I would again lose her to another location.

Guenther also liked me and even let me wear his expensive watch when I went to the movie with my friends. I'll never forget returning home very late that evening, and my family thinking that I had been afraid to return for fear that I had lost his watch. Actually, we sat through the movie twice, and I hadn't lost the watch, but was sent to bed early anyway without supper. Both Rosel and Guenther sneaked up to my room with a sandwich, as they were feeling sorry for me. It didn't surprise me when my mother, not knowing this, also tiptoed into my room with something to eat half an hour later.

I intensely loved my sister, and when I discovered months later that she was pregnant with my niece Beate, I couldn't hold back how delighted I was for her. I realized that this would change our relationship now that she would be dividing her affections between her new daughter, her husband, and myself, but I couldn't help but share in her excitement. Of course, being an aunt at the tender age of thirteen added to the anticipation of achieving celebrity status among my friends.

Life, however, continued to deal harshly with Rosel, as Beate was separated from both parents at birth due to their continuing struggle with Tuberculosis. As a result, my new niece was placed in isolation in a Berlin hospital with no one to provide the warm hugs and toys so desperately essential to an infant. For nine months, the nurses only permitted my sister to look at her new daughter through a window, and restricted communications between the two of them by requiring them to use only hand waving motions. Finally, after the nine month isolation period, Beate was released, but not to her parents, whose condition had worsened, but to my parents who, in their fifties were ill equipped to handle a nine month old infant. Eventually this set of events resulted in Beate being raised by her grandmother in conjunction with limited support from Rosel.

We kept Beate with us in Quedlinburg for six months, during which time Rosel's health improved as the open tuberculosis closed. Her husband's continued to worsen, however, resulting in his being sent to a sanatorium in the mountains. Guenther Glorius died in 1954 without ever having held his child, and my sister, 30 years old at the time, never married again. My little niece, Beate, in the meantime, having spent her early months with nothing but her hands and fingers with which to play, spent most of her hours during the day continuing to stare into space while the intertwining of her tiny fingers—her only form of entertainment.

Quedlinburg-my great grandparents' house

Quedlinburg-center of town

My Father and his brothers:(L to R): Hans, Pappi, Kurt, Guenther

My father on the Russian front-1940

My father on the Russian Front-1940

Father at Normandy 1944

Father at Normandy 1944

Father (white coat) back in Russia

My father in formal dress uniform-1943

Father just before his death-1953

My Mother -1926 at the age of 24 (white dress)

Mother in 1952 at the age of 50

Me at the age of 5

Erich with his paintings in Heidelberg-1958

Erich, Rosel, and I in 1975

Rosel and I in 1985

My husband, David, and I in 1995

My Escape from East Germany

CHAPTER XIV
Survival Under Communism

Living conditions remained very sordid and food became a more and more difficult commodity to obtain. My mother, still bartering her sewing with the Russian soldiers in exchange for food, had been given heirlooms handed down for generations within her family consisting mostly of jewelry imbedded with small clusters of garnets. Those stones eventually provided our subsistence. One by one she would pick the stones from her necklace or bracelet and exchange them for eggs and some sort of fat from the neighboring farmers. Somehow she managed to mix a strange concoction of this substance along with rice and flour to form one of the most disagreeable combinations one could imagine. It truly tasted awful, but it apparently provided the much needed fat, which she insisted was very nourishing for our bodily systems. Of course Erich, as usual, found this to be an appetizing dish, but anything at all which was remotely related to food served him well. I'll never forget losing my appetite watching her skin the rabbit a farmer had given us. Being a poor eater anyway, I readily gave my portion to Erich who very agreeably devoured every morsel.

The temptation to steal food eventually graduated into stealing other items. First the eggs from the farmers' chicken coops and apples from the local orchards. Later tobacco from the corner store for the father of one of my close friends. Unfortunately, my mother found out about that particular incident and made me return to the store to admit my guilt. This resulted in my having to wash the floor in that store for two weeks.

At the age of twelve I had matured enough to steal the writings of Honre de Balzac from the local bookstore. His writings during that era were considered to be true pornography. How exciting going to bed with my flashlight under the covers reading those titillating tales by Balzac until being discovered by my mother. She stripped me of the book, but Erich, always my benefactor, convinced her to give it back since I was determined to read it anyway.

Probably one of the more memorable experiences for me under our illustrious Communist leaders took place when the elite officials of the DDR, including Walter Ulbricht himself, the statesman and president of the German Democratic Republic, honored us with his presence. It should be stated from the onset, so that I don't incriminate myself, that all children of school age were required to belong to some sort of Communist youth organization affiliated with the Free German Youth. This was the Communist version of Nazi Germany's Hitler Youth. My, how original all of these fascist bureaucracies seemed to be. I looked upon my association with the Young Pioneers no differently than a Girl Scout today views her troop association.

As I stated earlier, I was considered somewhat brash, outspoken, and the "tomboy" of the group, and therefore, was assigned the honor of making a floral presentation to President Ulbricht on behalf of the Young Pioneers of Quedlinburg. An opportunity many would have sought, but not I.

Knowing how much my father hated the Communists and realizing that the last thing he would ever want to witness was his 12 year-old daughter walking onto a stage and graciously presenting a bunch of flowers to the ruthless leader of Communist Germany, I was tempted to decline the honor. On the other hand, there was also the possibility that my father wouldn't be there, since he was supposed to be at his factory working. I could always use the excuse, in the event of being seen, that turning down this opportunity might anger the Stasi, and in turn get my family in all sorts of trouble. Little did I realize that when Ulbricht comes to town all places of work are shut down, and everyone is compelled to appear at the festivities. Another paid holiday for the working man under the totally unproductive Communist regime.

There was a great deal of fanfare when they called me to the stage to make the presentation. Very politely, with my nerves in a state of frenzy, I strode up to our president and handed him the flowers as he thankfully planted a gentle kiss on the top of my head. As casually as I possibly could while I was on the platform I scanned the audience attempting to verify that Pappi wasn't anywhere to be seen. I returned to my seat with a great sense of relief knowing that he was nowhere in sight.

That evening when I walked in the house, my father, in one of his more playful moods, asked me how I spent my day. After I danced around the issue for a while, he commented that he saw a little girl that looked just like me today up on the stage with our illustrious president. So much for the idea of not getting caught. Fortunately, he also was only too aware of the possible consequences of my turning down the chance to make the presentation, and could do nothing but smile. Thank God!

By my fourteenth birthday in 1952, the time had arrived for me to get serious about my life and my future. The system called for me to make decisions that would affect the direction, if any, my destiny would turn. Customarily in Europe, at that age, one had to choose between an education leading towards a trade, or one leading to higher education focusing on the liberal arts and sciences. In other words, trade school versus the university. Frequently, the decision wasn't made by the student but by her educators. In all honesty, I had no strong feelings one way or the other and had no problem letting someone else make that decision for me.

Considering my academic achievements had been somewhat limited, and the fact that I lived in an area famous for its ability to grow and nurture botanical seeds, which were exported throughout the entire world, I chose to specialize in botany in a trade school. The fact that Quedlinburg was the center of botanical research for Germany, due to its unusually fertile soils, had always intrigued me, and to this day my love for creating flowering gardens and the study of plants dominates the vast majority of my time. So, in what direction would you think that our wonderful system would guide me? The "State" in its all-knowing wisdom sent me to the neighboring town of Thalle to learn mechanics, so I could go into my father's business.

The schedule they established was quite simple in the eyes of the authorities. I would continue to live at the school in Quedlinburg where I was boarding, get up at 4:00am three days a week and ride the train to Thalle, where I operated a drill press. The other three days I would continue to attend school and work on developing my athletic skills while training to be an Olympic track star for the glory of the DDR. When I was lucky, they permitted me to stop by to see my parents one day a week, otherwise only when I could sneak away for a quick visit. Although this agenda seemed very clear in the minds of the school directors, it seemed equally clear in my own mind that this schedule would be terminated by me shortly after learning what being a drill press operator was all about. Within a time span of a few weeks I managed to get excused from the program, using the special treatment I received as a potential athlete for the republic. Although the sports training part of my life had begun to wear thin with me, it did provide me with special privileges.

Athletics started to take more and more of my time. Although the initial excitement associated with travelling to Leipzig, Berlin, and other East block cities had its upside, it got old very quickly. Gradually we were forced to become more regimented and the pressure to improve our performance steadily increased. Although not inclined to bend to such rigor, I realized that my athletic ability provided the key to certain liberties that the state granted me.

CHAPTER XV
My Father's Sudden Passing

One of the few pleasures that my father allowed himself was the thrill of bicycling through the Harz Mountains. It seemed to be his only release from the oppression that weighed so heavily on our family. Occasionally, he permitted me to accompany him on these excursions which provided me with those few moments I needed for the two of us become reacquainted. Unfortunately, his invitations were rare, so most of his cycling was done solo.

It was one such Sunday ride, when he wanted to be alone as he rode through the rugged mountains, that the doctors concluded to be more than he could handle. The unusually warm and humid conditions caused him to stop along the way for a swim in one of the spring fed mountain lakes to cool off. I remember him describing the refreshing feeling of walking into the cold blue water. The tiny lake only the size of a few city blocks surrounded by evergreens and nestled between two mountain peaks reminded him of an oasis in the desert.

When he returned home abnormally exhausted, he immediately went to lie down on the couch in the living room. I'll never forget how pale he appeared to be and how weak his voice sounded as he told us about his latest escapades while winding through the mountainous roads.

He spent that night on the living room couch simply too exhausted to make the walk up the stairs to his bedroom. My mother covered him with a blanket and the family, then consisting of Erich, my mother, and I (Rosel being in Berlin), went to bed. We all woke up early the next morning after a sleepless night caused by our concern for my father. When I arrived downstairs in the living room where he had spent the night on the couch, my mother was already by his side attending to him. He had developed a fever while having great difficulty moving his toes. Later that day the paralysis invaded his legs.

Now I have often been told that the disease poliomyelitis can be caused by over-activity in extreme heat followed by a sudden cooling down by jumping into cold water. I've never known whether or not this is an "old wives' tale," a common form of conveying information in my family, or a proven medical fact. I later learned that polio is an infectious viral disease of the central nervous system that paralyzes the muscles including those that were required for my father to breathe.

Erich, home for the weekend from Dresden where he had been studying art, looked the symptoms up in some sort of home remedy book and immediately diagnosed the polio even before the doctor arrived. Unfortunately, he had diagnosed the symptoms correctly. He also packed his bags and left at once for Dresden, as he read that the contiguousness of the disease required that a quarantine would be placed on the house as well as on its occupants. Erich had no desire to be trapped in Quedlinburg for any length of time, being overly anxious to get back to his studies. Having received a grant from the finest art institute in

Germany, and being so devoted to his courses, he determined that nothing would interfere with his ultimate dream of becoming one of Europe's great twentieth century artists.

The doctors first moved my father to our local hospital a few miles from the house. My mother and I occasionally rode our bikes in violation of the quarantine restrictions to visit under his window. The ride only took fifteen to twenty minutes, but we enjoyed the time together. The flowers that bordered the roadside paths always lifted our spirits as we often stopped to notice the newly budding roses and smell the fragrance of some of the more unique varieties that graced the front yards of many homes along the way. Just before arriving at the hospital we followed a path through a vacant field covered with every sort of wild flower imaginable. Now and then we would stop to pick lilacs as we marveled at the setting of this flowered field nestled in the middle of the mountain scenery. Little wonder why my home in Quedlinburg is still so dear to me.

When we arrived under his window Pappi, with a great deal of effort, raised his upper body slightly off the bed in order to see us as the nurse pulled aside the drapes. My last memories of him were the motions he made to my mother, who apparently blocked me from his view, to step aside so he could better observe his youngest daughter. By now, paralyzed from the hips down, he had a good notion that this might be his last chance to see me. It seemed that he tried in those last few moments to make amends for his lifelong aloof temperament, and the time spent away from his children.

Late one night after returning from the hospital a sad reunion took place when I heard a familiar whistle beneath my window. It took only two notes for me to recognize the sound, and I jumped out of bed to greet her. Rosel had heard of my father's condition and brought Beate down from Berlin to visit. The thought of seeing Rosel again as I threw open the shutters of my bedroom window and looked down into the street below couldn't have thrilled me more. Due to the quarantine, she wasn't permitted in the house, but it was so good to see her even from a distance. We talked for nearly two hours, Rosel standing in the unlit street under my bedroom window holding Beate and me in my pajamas straining to get a better look at both of them.

As we filled each other in on what had been going on in our lives during the past few years I couldn't help but drag up the images that had branded themselves to my mind of my sister's ordeal while being held in captivity by the Stasi. It felt so comforting to sit at my window and just talk with her about our experiences and express our feelings and hopes about the future. I brought her up to date regarding Pappi and told her that things were not looking very bright for his recovery. She, in turn, talked of Beate and the bright lights of Berlin compared to dark and dingy Quedlinburg and other cities in the East through which she had traveled on her train ride home. She stayed with our neighbors that night and returned to Berlin the next day. Her short visit did so much to brighten my frame of mind and strengthen my resolve to escape from the political morass of the East.

Only three iron lungs were available in East Germany at that time. These devices provided the only mechanical means to assist a paralyzed lung to breathe. Located in Leipzig, Magdeburg, and Halle all were being utilized when my father took ill. The one in Halle finally freed up when its patient died, thereby providing my father with the opportunity to become its next patron. His departure from the Quedlinburg hospital is burned into my memory, as his gesture, when looking out of his window and waving my mother out of the way so he could see me, was the last view I had of him alive. He died three days after being transferred to Halle, only one week after his fateful bike ride through the Harz Mountains.

The notification I received of his death was unusually cruel and abrupt. While riding my bicycle around the city, again in violation of the quarantine, Mrs. Lebow, our housekeeper, unceremoniously stopped me. She grabbed my bike by the handlebars and very harshly told me to go straight home "because your father is dead." I proceeded to ride straight home in a state of shock with tears streaming down my face clouding my vision. The ride home seemed to last forever, and my heart felt as if it would never regain its wholeness. I grieved for a man I hardly knew, even though he was my father.

Because Pappi was well known throughout the area, the East Germans, in their unmatched capability to deliver the propaganda message, declared in the local newspaper that his death was a result of the West German food being sent to him by his daughter, Rosel, from Berlin. Only the mind of the Stasi could put my father's death to such inhumanely good use in promoting their unsavory cause.

CHAPTER XVI
My Delinquent Mother

Routine life continued throwing debris in my path, so I wasn't terribly surprised, after my father's death, about the changes that seemed to overwhelm the family. With Rosel and Beate living in Berlin, Erich studying his art in Dresden, I continued in my endeavor to compete in the Junior East European Olympics. This, of course, involved going to school, living in the dormitory, and traveling to different cities occasionally to compete in the high jump and broad jump.

It started with my mother, being alone again, only now with no hope for a husband to return from the war. Her friends continued to drop by and visit her, but most of them weren't the coffee klatch type. Wine and whiskey seemed to keep their friendships alive. As a result, Mother started drinking a bit more than usual in order to maintain her new friendships, as well as pass the time of day. Somewhere along the line, either from the influence of her friends, or from sheer boredom, she encouraged me to start meeting boys. For all I know, this may have been some sort of vicarious means to satisfy her own loneliness. This for me, at the age of 16, should not have been unusual; however, as the proverbial tomboy, I was frankly more interested in my high jump competition, and the travel associated with competing in the East Block.

At some point the obvious was bound to occur, as it did one day while returning on the train from a track and field event in East Berlin. He was three years older than I and the subject of fantasies for the other girls on the track team. Although certainly flattered by his attention as he made a point of coming over to talk with me, I tried to appear somewhat indifferent to his smooth introduction. My teammate sitting next to me gave up her seat in order for this young man to make himself more comfortable while trying to engage me in conversation. Being my usual flirtatious self, I viewed Rudy Wambera as a challenge rather than the object of a future romance. Keep in mind, that I was a very immature sixteen, unlike a sixteen-year-old of the 21st century. Rudy, the son of displaced persons who had been moved from the former Sudetenland to a caserne, or converted army barracks, outside of Quedlinburg sometime after the war, effortlessly engaged me in conversation. We discovered that we both lived in Quedlinburg, which may have seemed convenient; however, as our dialogue progressed, his luster slowly waned.

Rudy and I had very little in common, so we talked about sports, and what it was like to travel around the East Block countries competing with other girls who had Olympic ambitions. He acted somewhat interested in what I was saying; however, his mind seemed to be preoccupied more with my looks than my conversation. After a rather boring two hours on the train, we arrived in Quedlinburg where I happily said my good-byes hoping that I had seen the last of him. Unfortunately, Rudy Wambera ultimately became a living nightmare for me during the following months.

Somehow, probably from one of my girlfriends, Rudy found out my address that I had refused to provide him while on the train. Two or three days later he came knocking at my door, and I must admit I was a both surprised and even flattered. I guess I'd never thought much about boys at that stage of my life, let alone a ***man*** of 19-years-old. I asked him to come in the house to meet my mother. This may have either been a fatal error in judgement, or something that had already been predetermined in the malicious minds of the Stasi.

As the three of us sat in our living room talking about nothing very interesting, it became noticeable to me that I was slowly becoming somewhat of a non-entity as the conversation progressed. I assumed, of course, that my being a young teen-ager among adults made me less interesting to the exchange taking place between Rudy and my mother. Mother, on the other hand, appeared quite interested in Rudy's background as he proceeded to talk of his parents moving the family from the Sudetenland to Germany. Strangely enough, it seemed that Rudy took quite a curious interest in whatever my mother was talking about. Later in the relationship between the three of us, it became clear that both my mother and Rudy had entirely different motives for their respective levels of interest.

I felt relieved when Rudy finally departed that day, as I no longer considered him a challenge and clearly had no interest in him. Conversely, my mother couldn't get over what a nice young man he appeared to be and strongly encouraged me to continue seeing him. Because of my mother's influence, and Rudy Wambera's persistence, he continued to come around the house feigning an interest in me while my mother continued to promote our relationship with an overly zealous support. In my own naivete, I honestly had no idea of the clandestine nature of the relationship that was developing between this scoundrel and my mother.

Things started to become clear one day when Mommy suggested that the three of us take the train to Berlin to visit Rosel. I had a difficult time understanding the logic of dragging Rudy on this trip, particularly since he had never even met Rosel. I simply shrugged and agreed to the arrangement because I had no choice, and I didn't want to stay home by myself. It seemed that my mother was in the process of attempting to make Rudy Wambera part of the Spannaus family regardless of my growing distaste for him.

As the three of us wandered down the famous Kurfürstendamm, Berlin's extravagant shopping street, similar to the Magnificent Mile in Chicago, I peeked in one of the windows and saw real nylon stockings. Oh, what I would have done to have those, even just one pair. When I turned to Mommy and pleaded for her to make the purchase, she simply ignored me, saying that we were not on a shopping trip. Not fifteen minutes later, while on the way to Rosel's apartment Rudy stopped to look longingly at a pair of motorcycle glasses. Without the slightest hesitation my mother marched into the shop and bought them for this clown.

Not being a shy wallflower, I immediately confronted Mother in tears and asked, "What the hell is going on here?" Mommy simply shrugged and gave no response. When we arrived at Rosel's apartment, with tears still visible on my face, I related the whole incident to my big sister, who simply stated that "Mommy was up to her usual games again." By that time I had become fed up with both my mother and Rudy Wambera, and could think of nothing I'd rather do than head for home.

The problem continued to persist even once we returned to Quedlinburg, as my mother continued to promote my relationship with Rudy, a relationship that began to repulse me, and of which I wanted no part. Not until I traveled to Warsaw for an overnight track and field competition did things begin to crystallize.

The track meet, scheduled to last three days, ended up being cut short due to some nasty weather that engulfed Poland all week. We returned home late the second day. I walked into the house around midnight and tiptoed to my room very quietly to avoid waking Mommy. Apparently too quietly, as the silence in my home was broken by voices coming from my mother's bedroom. Strange, I thought, considering Erich was in Dresden and Rosel was in Berlin, unless of course, one of them had decided to pay us a surprise visit. With my hopes high that this was the case, I opened Mommy's bedroom door and became overwhelmed with nausea when I beheld a sight that no daughter should ever witness. I froze as I watched the one and only Rudy Wambera quickly cover himself with a blanket as he lay in bed with my mother. A nearly empty bottle of whiskey on the nightstand.

My only feelings were that of total anger accompanied by blind rage. My stomach seemed to climb into the back of my throat as my mind became a blur of hate and anguish towards both of them. I felt no control over my emotions or my actions. I remember screaming in an uncontrollable frenzy while jumping on Rudy and dragging him off the bed. The tears streaming down my face blinded me. All of a sudden, Mommy's motives, in promoting the relationship between Rudy and myself, became quite clear. She began to pummel me with her fists while screaming; "Who do you think you are, interfering with my life?" I couldn't believe this ordeal happening to me, as I stood there in a state of utter shock and astonishment as she continued to beat on me. Even today, I can't find words to explain my feelings. Yet when my husband, David, asks me whether or not I really loved my mother, for some reason or another, I always answer yes.

How clearly the memory stays with me of how I ran to my father's bedroom, grabbed the picture of him in his army uniform and clutched it to my breast with tears literally streaming down my face. Never before had I considered the thought of self-destruction. But as I opened his third floor window and proceeded to climb out on the ledge, suicide became a viable escape. I don't really know whether or not I could have jumped, and even if I had, the fall from that height would probably have just broken a few bones. Before I could even think that far ahead I felt a firm hand clamp onto my arm, as Mr. Lebow pulled me inside the window.

The nightmare was not yet finished. Mommy ran into the room holding brass knuckles she had probably obtained from our mutual friend, Mr. Wambera, and took a swipe at my face before being subdued by Mr. Lebow. Obviously in a drunken frenzy, she was in no state with which to be reasoned. Without giving much thought to anything, I quickly ran down the stairs and over to my school dormitory. The chief administrator, Mrs. Knoble, had no idea why I would be returning to the dorm since the weekend was just starting and the local students were all permitted to spend the time off at home. She simply took one look at my expression of determination and the tears flooding my face and decided it was best not to ask any questions that night.

Earlier I stated that my mother and Rudy had entirely different motives for their respective interests in each other. Mother's interest was obviously sexual companionship. I learned later, however, that Rudy Wambera had more complex and evil intents in developing his attentiveness towards my mother.

CHAPTER XVII

The Black Market and Rudy the Informer

Much of the truth came out the following morning when the police came to my school to have a private discussion with me. They took me to an isolated room in the schoolhouse and sat me down as though I had committed some sort of felony. In fact a crime had taken place, but it had to do with my mother not me. The police informed me that they had arrested her in regards to her involvement with a black market operation being conducted between East Germany and West Berlin.

It seems that a Jewish survivor of one of the concentration camps, David Warshamsky, befriended Rosel during her new life in Berlin. Mr. Warshamsky had been seeking a contact in the East to distribute watches that he obtained from a West German source still unknown to me. David and his partner collaborated in a black market scheme whereby he funneled these watches, a rare commodity in the East, through a trusted conduit, my mother for one, in exchange for a 50-50 split of the profits. In addition to a share of the profits he provided her with cigarettes and coffee from the West, of much higher quality than the garbage sold anywhere behind the Iron Curtain. Mommy couldn't pass up the cigarettes and coffee to which she had become nearly addicted, and the extra money was used to feed us.

Rosel, completely unaware of David Warshamsky's activities because of his generosity towards her, was anxious to introduce him to my mother during one of her visits. No romantic relationship existed between Rosel and David. They simply shared some mutually horrible experiences during and after the war at the hands of the German government and became close platonic friends. After their introduction it seemed strange to me that Mommy made so many trips to Berlin to visit Rosel. Later it became apparent that she used this as an excuse to make the exchange with Warshamsky. She brought him the cash from her sales while picking up more merchandise to distribute.

She once made the very costly mistake of taking our mutual friend Wambera, not only to Berlin, but also to Warshamsky's very secret location. This site, I later discovered, was a run down tenement in the poorer section of West Berlin that could be entered through a peephole door similar to those secret Chicago speakeasy saloons that operated during prohibition. When Warshamsky opened the door to see that my mother had brought Rudy he was utterly enraged. He told her then and there that this stranger would bring about their downfall. That evening they proceeded to conduct their business, and within a matter of hours, he closed shop and disposed of the rest of his merchandise. Shortly afterwards he moved to Pirmasens in southern Germany where he used his new wealth to purchase a popular restaurant and bar frequented by American military officers stationed in nearby army posts. Known as the Atlantic Bar, it later came to play an important role in my own life.

It's no secret how the Stasi discovered my mother's role in the smuggling operation. Rudy Wambera was simply one of the paid informers used by the Stasi to uncover any activities that violated the East German protocol. Remember that the Stasi employed one informer for every 90 citizens. Rudy, not only used my mother for his own pleasure, but received rewards from the Stasi at the same time. Some might call that criminally resourceful; I considered it prostitution.

When the police informed me of my mother's predicament, I admit to being so disgusted because of her pampering attitude with Rudy, that even a ten year sentence in Siberia wouldn't have caused me to shed a tear on her behalf. At that time, I honestly didn't care if I ever saw her again in my life. In thinking about how she encouraged, and practically sponsored the relationship between that son of a bitch, Wambera, and myself for her own satisfaction, just to have an excuse to have him around, I felt deceived and totally betrayed. Surprising the two of them in bed together filled me with utter revulsion. It could only be true retribution that she incur the judgement and prison term she deserved for sleeping with a Stasi informer.

Several months after her imprisonment, Mommy told me that Rudy had threatened her safety if she didn't cooperate with him. I found that impossible to believe. It seems that, even today, Germans who lived through Hitler's regime, the Holocaust, and the Communist domination, are prone to making all sorts of excuses regarding both their past and present behavior. I must admit that I am guilty of this as well and need to be reminded from time to time that the world is filled with others who have suffered as intensely and simply don't have to rely on such hardship excuses for their conduct.

For me things seemed to be going downhill quickly and a state of depression filled my insides. With Erich in Dresden, Rosel in Berlin, Mommy in the local prison, and my father deceased, I was left to take care of myself. As a seventeen-year old female living in a police state where no one could be trusted, I didn't feel prepared to handle the circumstances. I desperately needed some person or some activity to refocus my thinking and provide a glimmer of hope to which I could cling. At this point the only activities with which I could most easily associate were the botanical training that I loved, the track and field competition which I tolerated, and the loneliness that surrounded me like a dense fog. The fact that the Stasi watched my every move for some time to come also provided me with no small sense of fear.

The school decided to make me a permanent resident of the dormitory in nearby Wettersleben. For some reason, about which I'm not clear, they scheduled me to attend agricultural classes three days a week in the Wettersleben branch and three days in Quedlinburg, returning each night to the dorms in Wettersleben. As bad as the conditions were in the Quedlinburg dormitories, they were absolutely horrible in Wettersleben, a real dump, with dreadful food and filthy rooms.

My thoughts of why my life had become so complicated made me think soberly about how I could begin to change the outcome rather than continue floating aimlessly like the debris of a shipwreck in the ocean. Bitterness seemed to be overtaking my life and I permitted it without so much as putting up any resistance. The appalling conditions in Wettersleben convinced me at that point to contest and no longer tolerate the situation.

During the second week I packed my belongings, a few clothes that would easily fit into a knapsack, and gingerly climbed out the first floor window next to my bed in the Wettersleben dormitory. It was a drizzly, cold night as I walked the streets of the tiny village with no idea where my next stop would be. I recall being hypnotized by reflections from shiny wet cobblestones as I trudged along aimlessly determined that I had spent my last night in that squalid dorm. The streets were empty, as the shops had closed several hours earlier. Again, my feelings of loneliness overwhelmed me, being the only living sole wandering about at midnight in this small community. After roaming the narrow streets for about an hour, a small vehicle pulled alongside and the driver, a custodian of the school, demanded that I get into the car immediately. My escape had obviously interrupted his night's sleep and his voice reflected his nasty mood.

After running away on five separate occasions, and sneaking into my old Quedlinburg dormitory, the authorities reassigned me permanently to Quedlinburg, as they knew that this pattern was not about to change.

Just prior to my mom's trial, she was being held temporarily in the local prison. I remember going to the bridge which served as a traffic overpass of the muddy stream that passed through the city. Standing on one of the parapets, I had a good view of Mommy's prison window on the third story of the ugly stone building. I always had the ability to emit a whistle so piercing that anyone within a hundred meters would know it was mine. It's a talent I still have today and still use to call my dogs and my husband.

As I stood on the bridge and let out the shrill sound, Mommy immediately knew I had come. As we waved our handkerchiefs back and forth to each other, I truly felt bothered by my mixed emotions. Here my mother was being held in jail as a common criminal, and I sensed that morally I should be sympathetic towards her. On the other hand, I held her in such contempt for her recent behavior with Rudy, that I simply felt no compassion and didn't even care about what type of punishment she received. I had to ask myself, what kind of a daughter would feel so callous towards her own mother?

A trial had been scheduled for the following week, and a local city official told me that I would be asked to testify. Unlike the court system in America, where a family member is not required to testify against their mother or father, this was Communist East Germany where people were encouraged to betray their closest friends and relatives. As it happened, her behavior had so upset me that I actually looked forward to furnishing the police with whatever testimony it took to provide the appropriate penalties.

The first item on my agenda was a visit to the beauty shop, where I told the stylist to make me look as old and mature as possible. I wanted to be a credible looking witness, if nothing else. The beautician complied by very carefully combing my hair straight back styling it into a bun. I swear she must have aged my appearance by three to five years, which surprised and pleased both of us no end. The next episode was completely unplanned.

I returned home from the beauty shop and developed a torturous headache with pain like I had never in my life experienced. The suffering was so agonizing and the spasms so sharp that death would have seemed a more merciful relief. This happened to be the first in a series of excruciating migraine and cluster headaches that plagued me for the next forty years of my life. On several occasions, following such an occurrence, I required two to three weeks of hospitalization time in total isolation while doctors experimented with an untold number of drugs attempting to relieve the agony. Nothing ever worked and eventually the headaches would subside on their own after fifteen to twenty days.

I remember someone calling for Dr. Zodke, our family physician, who administered an injection and ordered me into a private room in the hospital. Private rooms, let me remind you, were totally unheard of in East Germany in those days. Most hospital quarters were the ward variety housing eight to ten patients in one ward.

The following day the local prosecuting attorney in my mother's upcoming trial came to visit me in the hospital. My feelings at that point consisted of the severe pain from my persistent headache matched only by the intense desire to get even with Mommy. Without any hesitation I told him everything I knew regarding the relationship between Rudy and my mother including the watch smuggling, and Mommy's attempt to encourage a romance between Rudy and myself.

As it turned out, Dr. Zodke, in my room at the time, witnessed my shocking diatribe that caught him quite off guard. Astonished by my disclosures and out of deference for our family, which still carried a level of respect even then, he came to an agreement with the prosecutor: I should not be released from the hospital to provide the damning testimony that I had just revealed. The prosecutor reluctantly went along with him.

Despite the fact that I was not permitted to testify, they had enough evidence from our mutual friend, the real villain, Rudy Wambera, to sentence my mother to five years in the Thuringen prison, over 200 kilometers from home. One would have thought that by this time my feelings would have mellowed, and a small amount of sympathy may have crept into my emotions regarding my mother's consequences. But I had become so hardened by the entire situation, that I still felt neither remorse nor sympathy.

CHAPTER XVIII
Alone

I suppose my only true feelings were quite selfish. I was now really alone. With our house locked up and off limits to me, the authorities sent me to a trade school in Ditfurt, 20 kilometers from Quedlinburg, to study botany and landscaping. My only possession of any value at this time, other than the clothes I took with me, was a key to our house. The police attempted to make certain that no one would have access to the Spannaus home on Breite Strasse and proceeded to lock all of the entrances and gather the outstanding keys. They hadn't realized that I had slipped an extra key into my book bag before leaving.

Erich, still going to school in Dresden, asked me to come there to live with him in his tiny one room apartment. I had been there once before, and to even call it an apartment extolled an undeserved level of flattery upon the dwelling, as it more closely resembled a one room garret that starving artists call home. As much as I loved my brother, there was no way that he could convince me to share that squalor with him. What's more, he was having a difficult enough time providing enough food for himself. As long as I had the opportunity to live off of the "State," I preferred being alone in school.

Another alternative opened up that came through an offer from my Uncle Hans, now managing a clothing store in Kalbe. At one point he owned the store, however, under our new regime it became state owned property, and he was graciously permitted to operate it. How generous of our local authorities. Under the circumstances, I considered the offer of Uncle Hans and Aunt Trude very generous, particularly since I really didn't want to be left completely alone at this point in my life.

After a tense two-hour train ride to Kalbe, where my uncle met me at the depot, I felt relieved to be with relatives once again. The relief, however, was short lived, as life with my aunt and uncle did not even approach my expectations. As a matter of fact, instead of being treated as a guest who had recently experienced some extremely traumatic events, they looked upon me as more of a servant to do their bidding and cleaning up after them. Their son, Hans Joachim, one year older than I, was the total focal point of their attention, while I became the Cinderella of the household, there to perform the menial chores.

Not only did I feel so very isolated in their home; I became a total stranger in the city with no friends and no one within miles with whom I could even confide. In essence, virtually an outcast with no safe harbor. After spending one week in this environment, I returned to the school in Ditfurt, where at least I wasn't a complete unknown, and a bit closer to my Quedlinburg home.

Now I began to understand my aloneness. My most comfortable choice meant remaining in the Ditfurt trade school whose athletic department virtually owned me. I was simply another asset in their inventory of athletes, required to do their bidding on command. Oddly enough, after a few months I didn't really mind the routine that much, and started taking advantage of several activities. Dances were held in conjunction with the other schools in the area, and I actually started looking forward to the traveling associated with our sports events held in other cities. The fact that those who were involved in athletics received special treatment suited me just fine.

Then came the loneliest days of my entire life, the Christmas holidays break. Even today, when the Christmas period approaches, I get that gnawing feeling of aloneness, as I think back on the Christmas of 1955. I had no place to go, no one to visit, and no one with which to even share a Christmas dinner. Erich was away from Dresden visiting friends, Rosel was too far away in Berlin, and Mommy was in the Thuringen prison.

As my classmates and teammates at Ditfurt were all packing to return home for Christmas, they asked what my plans were for the holidays. Not that they really cared, but they were trying to be polite. Being a very proud soul, and ashamed to admit that I had no place to go, I bravely responded that I had several invitations to visit friends, and wasn't sure which one I would honor with my presence. I ended up telling them that I intended to visit my brother in Dresden, and even feigned going to the train station to buy a ticket.

For me it resembled facing the world in your most embarrassing attire and admitting that you have no friends and no place to turn; The response from the world, nothing but a sigh of boredom. I was overcome with a wretched feeling of sadness and indescribable depression.

In returning to Quedlinburg, thankful for the fact that I had kept a key to my home, I planned to hibernate there alone for the holidays. The State now in possession of the house, assigned the Lebows, living in one of our apartments, the role caretakers. I sneaked into my parents' quarters and pulled all of the shades and closed the drapes, so I could remain undetected by any passers-by. Having purchased two loaves of bread and canned chicken broth, I was prepared to barricade myself in for the next ten days. A candle to heat the broth served as my stove, and I made certain that it was lit only during daylight hours so the flickering light could not be seen from the outside.

One day, just prior to Christmas, I couldn't resist the urge to venture forth from hiding and walk around my beloved city of Quedlinburg. As it turned out, I ran into one of my mother's closest friends. The families had become so close over the years that I called her "Tanta Hanna," Aunt Hanna, although she wasn't a blood relative. I only know that my mother had done many favors for her during the course of their friendship. I was so desperate not to be alone on Christmas that I summoned all the courage within me, putting aside any pride that was left, and asked her if she would have me come for Christmas dinner. Her response left me devastated. She said that she already had too many guests coming and couldn't handle one more. With that, I returned home and cried for several hours as I thought of how unkind and thoughtless people could really be.

The next seven days were spent in the house reading, listening to my father's records, and eating dried bread and soup. I didn't dare go out on the streets again. When I returned to school, I told everyone what a wonderful time I had had visiting my brother in Dresden. I probably didn't fool anyone.

CHAPTER XIX
Preview to Freedom

As time passed, living within the confines of the school became very routine and quite dreary. I had started my fourth year and nothing seemed to change: three days each week spent in the classroom followed by three days in the field getting practical botanical experience. Of course, the track and field training and travel to the different events tended to break the monotony, but the trips to Berlin for some of the meets began to take on a different meaning. In the back of my mind, I visualized that, having seen the lights of Berlin, a better life existed, with a better place to live it.

Family had also become a real concern, as I often wondered how we could have become so separated, and what it would take to get us together again. With Mommy in prison, Erich in Dresden, Rosel in Berlin, and me in Quedlinburg, it seemed wrong that a family that had lived through so much together could have drifted so far apart.

My athletic abilities allowed me to perform in several different events. Although I specialized in the high jump, I also competed in the broad jump, shot put, and 400 meter run. The volleyball team, however, provided my incentive for a better life since many of these competitions took place in Berlin. The motivation to excel for the glory of my Communist run school had become secondary to the desire to remain on the team in order to visit the stimulating surroundings in that city. I frequently reminisced about my previous visits to Rosel and how totally absorbed I had become with the vitality which embraced West Berlin. The bright lights, the constant feeling of activity and the smiling faces of people as they hurried down the street to shop at the magnificent department stores or meet in their favorite restaurants for lunch. Berlin symbolized a vibrant aliveness of freedom and an escape from the doldrums of the East German prison state.

With Easter vacation fast approaching I wrote a letter to Rosel asking if I could come to Berlin for the week to visit her. This took place, of course, five years before the infamous Berlin Wall had been erected when travel between East and West Berlin was relatively common. Unfortunately, Rosel wrote me that she would be away for the week, but suggested that I come anyway and stay at her apartment. This event signaled the major turning point in my life.

Having saved most of the stipend I received from the state as a reward for my athletic participation, and with some money Rosel had left for me, I arrived in Berlin like a small child with a fortune to spend on goodies not available in the East. Things like chocolates, fancy blouses, and nylon stockings. For one week I roamed the streets of West Berlin window shopping for clothes, electrical appliances like toasters and portable radios, and food that people in the East couldn't even conceive existed.

At night I could walk freely down Berlin's famous Kurfürstendamm, the equivalent of Broadway in New York and delight in the bright lights, the throngs of cheerful shoppers, and the outdoor restaurants, where I could stop and linger over a dish of raspberry ice cream. My God, how could there be such a wonderful place so close to the wearisome confines a few miles away? It was impossible to even imagine that this divided city could harbor such drastic contrast.

In East Berlin, the dark unlit streets were void of any shoppers or even those who wanted to take an evening stroll after dinner. The buildings had not been restored since the bombings during the war. Darkness even existed within the homes and apartments, due to a limited supply of power. Once evening engulfed East Berlin, people migrated back to their homes, and the streets remained empty until the next morning when they grudgingly plodded off to work.

The farther east one went, the heavier the night air became with the thick brown smoke created by the high sulfur coal used for heating. How bleak life could really be. And to think that this was my every day existence, with the few exceptions that occurred during my visits to Rosel.

Several weeks later, our volleyball team again traveled to play one of the East Berlin teams. Having arrived there a day early, I tried to convince my friend, Bimbo, to sneak away with me during our free time to visit my sister. Bimbo, even at the age of eighteen had already become the matronly submissive lemming unwilling to fight the Communist system. With her dark hair pulled back in braids, she turned her husky build towards me and gave me a grimace as though I had lost my mind. Terrified at the thought of going over the border, she told me in no uncertain terms that I was on my own. Only after describing the excitement of life in the West and the luxuries that were available, did she reluctantly agree to follow me. We took the S-bahn to West Berlin. Bimbo couldn't believe her eyes once we disembarked the train. After stuffing ourselves with chocolates and ice cream, we spent the night with Rosel and sneaked back to East Berlin bright and early the next morning in time for the match.

To provide you with some idea of this contrast, I took my daughter, Shirley, to visit Quedlinburg in the early 1970's, twenty years after my delinquent excursions with Bimbo. Occasionally we witnessed long lines of shoppers outside of some of the markets. Out of curiosity, we joined one of the waiting crowds. To our amazement, the people who had been waiting in line for hours were rewarded with a recent shipment of potatoes. They weren't even fresh. Things that Shirley took for granted when doing her window shopping in Wisconsin weren't even visible in store windows on the main street in Quedlinburg. An appliance store without one radio or television set displayed, a grocery store with nothing but a few boxes of crackers on the shelves, and clothing stores with naked mannequins.

During that same visit we were followed day and night by two men in leather coats, the Stasi. It seems that my name was still on the list of those who had escaped from the East, and my old Stasi friends wanted to make certain that my return would not create any subversive actions on the part of the locals. They certainly wanted to be sure that I had no intentions of initiating any clandestine activities. Although they didn't present any immediate problem for us, the thought of their constant presence proved to be quite distracting and at times even frightening.

After crossing Check Point Charlie as we returned to Berlin, Shirley admitted that she had never been so worried in her life. She did manage to maintain a very bold front during the entire time we were in the East. So effective was her masquerade that I had no idea until much later the extent to which fear had gripped her.

After my last visit to Rosel in 1956, I finally decided that I had had enough of the Stasi, enough of the command performances at sports events, enough of the forced appearances at demonstrations, and more than enough governmental controls directing my life. I had seen how the other half lived, and I wanted to be part of that half, regardless of what was involved to do it. My sister and my mother had suffered at the hands of the police and I wanted to make sure that I controlled my own future without the help of the State. My determination to simply get the hell out of this prison before it became inescapable incessantly occupied every sense in my body.

CHAPTER XX
Escape from Tyranny

The New Year celebration ringing in 1957 had also brought the good news of my mother's early release from prison. She returned home in January of that year, and after our long separation, I had forgiven her in my own mind. This did not mean that my deep-seated resentment of her didn't linger on, but I must admit I was terribly happy to be with her once more after nearly two years of being separated from my family.

Approaching my nineteenth birthday it felt like I had reached an earlier adulthood than most of my companions. Although we had all lived through the war, the Stasi, and the deprivation not experienced by our colleagues in the West, few had experienced the family turmoil and disruptions that had been thrust upon my loved ones and me. I considered myself an adult and determined to make the adult decision to leave this wretched existence in the East far behind.

The decision, although made in anger and frustration, had been derived from all of those conditions that made living in East Germany intolerable. Yes, I had seen the bright lights of Berlin and its contented inhabitants, but the thought of escape from tyranny far outweighed the thought of other alternatives: a release *from* rather than a flight *to*.

Two days after Mommy had arrived home I approached her with the ultimatum that I was leaving East Germany with or without my family. To my utter disbelief, she readily agreed with me and had expressed her own feelings towards our intolerable life form, saying she would proceed immediately to look for a way out—not an easy task.

I recalled the thousands of East Germans who had lost their lives in attempting to escape to the West. Those who had crawled through farm fields during the night in their attempt to cross the border but were cut down by snipers poaching in watchtowers. And those shot while furiously attempting to climb over the Berlin Wall. Many attempted to swim the muddy Spree River that separated freedom from imprisonment, while East German guards riddled the waters with machine gun bullets. Fathers throwing their children from buildings into the waiting arms of civilian rescuers on the other side of the border prior to the construction of the Wall and the creation of the "No Man's Land." There were those who took the trouble of concealing themselves in automobile gas tanks, or some that had spent years secretly hand digging tunnels under the border. I always admired the creative father who fabricated a hot air balloon from scrap material he'd saved for years and flew his entire family from Thuringen to somewhere in Bavaria.

These efforts represented the determination of a people seeking the escape to freedom with little consideration for the consequences. For many the consequences were certainly more severe than the risk. It's hard to estimate the number of East German citizens assassinated during their escape attempts and the even larger number thrown into prisons left there to languish, ultimately to be forgotten by their captors.

Mother had to be so very careful in making any arrangements for an escape, considering that the Stasi informers were everywhere, and would be rewarded for information leading to the interference and termination of such a venture.

First she contacted Erich, who had recently graduated from the Dresden School of Art. She wrote him a letter explaining the circumstances and urged him to return home so plans for the family's departure could be completed. To understand Erich's reaction requires an understanding of Erich.

He lived in his own world of art, and the regime under which he practiced his talent was of little consequence. Furthermore, his life as an artist in East Germany wouldn't demand quite the same effort to make a living as the competitive world that he'd read about on the other side of the Iron Curtain. He knew that the State would take care of him as long as he remained in the East and didn't become involved with any subversives. They only required that he create four paintings a year commissioned by the government. As a result, Erich resisted my mother' dictates and argued very strongly against leaving, but to no avail. Mommy made it very clear that she and I were leaving, and the

Communists would certainly make suffer any family members left behind. He had no choice, when she explained that the Stasi would most likely hold him responsible for our escape. She also told him that she would take care of him for as long as she lived. Another of my mothers broken promises.

Today, forty-five years later at the age of 79, Erich resides in a nursing home in West Berlin totally crippled by arthritis. Having lived his life as a starving artist, he still regrets his mother's decision to leave the East and take him along. Our mother has been deceased now for seventeen years, and he still demonizes her during our telephone conversations, regretting her decision to drag him from the comforts of the protective shell of Communism.

In retrospect, Erich probably should have remained in the East. Why should such a very gentle and artistic individual, afflicted with glandular problems that drove his weight well beyond his capability of moving with any agility, have been compelled to give up the only life style that provided him with any comfort and security? The poor guy even suffered the humiliation of being unable to grow facial hair. His smooth rosy complexion had never even required the use of a razor. By the age of sixty he developed severe crippling arthritis, forcing him to hold his paintbrush between the permanently curled index and ring fingers of his right hand. He couldn't bend over to pull on a pair of socks. Erich never married, and I honestly believe he has never made love to a woman.

He has lived by himself for most of his life, except for the short period he lived in a one-bedroom apartment shared with Rosel and my mother. Even now, a complete invalid, he lives alone in a nursing home in Berlin, from where he has no hope of ever leaving. It was Erich's dedication to the fine arts of music, painting, and writing that served as my incentive to attempt to understand the hidden beauty of the arts. Of course, he still berates Hitler as the monster who destroyed the world's way of life and idolizes Chairman Mao as the only one who had the capability of saving it.

Once Erich returned home, Mommy began the task of seeking a trustworthy source to mastermind our escape. She had to be so careful not to tip her hand to the wrong individual. It would take only one hint to such a person for my mother to find herself back in prison for the rest of her life. Eventually one of her trusted contacts introduced her to a man from Wettersleben who agreed to smuggle us out of East Germany one by one. Without any discussion or debate, Mommy told me that I would be the first to leave. I readily agreed and looked forward to the most exciting and dangerous opportunity of my life. Erich also approved of my going first as he hoped that if he waited long enough he might avoid the whole process.

The man assigned to take me out asked that I call him Mr. Munser. I'm sure he kept his real name a well concealed secret in the event that I would ever be questioned in the future. Regardless, it would be best for me to forget even his false name. Based upon the way he dressed, he looked much like a typical potato farmer in his early fifties with a very muscular build and dirty blond hair. He stood a little over six feet tall and I recall how his eyes, filled with suspicion, fit uncomfortably into his pockmarked complexion. I couldn't really decide just how much trust I could place in Munser but at this point it was of no consequence. The decision had been made.

From a very early age I frequently judged people by some rather unusual physical characteristics. I never trusted anyone with thin lips or short stubby fingers. In his favor Munser had long slender fingers with thick full lips. These features did provide me with a sense of comfort, although still somewhat limited.

Because the Stasi "black list" contained our family name as result of my mother's jail sentence, the cost for helping us flee had been escalated above the normal going price. This meant that my mother had to secretly sell some of our furniture and other belongings in order to raise enough cash to pay our guide. This had to be done very carefully to avoid raising any suspicions even among our closest friends.

Taking any sort of public transportation in those days involved a great deal of risk, as the police checked all personal papers and passports very closely when traveling by bus or train. Munser provided me with very precise instructions prior to departing. Take a small suitcase limited to one change of clothing and an extra pair of shoes for walking. Wear a warm jacket to conceal the additional underwear, light shirts, or sweater I chose to wear under my regular clothes. In the cool damp April of 1957 a warm coat wouldn't look that out of place. Whatever I could wear without looking suspicious would become my entire wardrobe once I entered the new world. The limited contents of my suitcase had to make it look like I intended to overnight at a friend's house in the event of a search. He further told me to put some food and bottled water in my suitcase.

As I stood listening to the directions from my new acquaintance, Munser, a very strange feeling came over me as I visualized the possible risks I would be undertaking during the next few days. As he described the plan with its inherent dangers of crawling between watchtowers in the darkness of night and sneaking through mine fields all alone before dawn broke, it almost seemed that he was attempting to plant seeds of doubt and anxiety in my mind. Would this cause me to reconsider the entire operation? Not on your life!

Instead, I felt exhilarated, knowing that I would finally be getting away from these surroundings and everything associated with them. At last I could relate to those who had spent years risking their lives to get out.

My thoughts had already gone beyond the escape process and focused on the bright lights of Berlin. What it would be like to have the freedom to choose my own way of life, with or without athletics. The idea that no one would be monitoring my every move and conversation brought a thrilling sensation to my insides. The opportunity to begin a completely new life in virtually a new world, gave me the will to take whatever risks were involved.

CHAPTER XXI
Good Bye Stasi

The cold April mist and fog, typical of the entire European continent at that time of year, surrounded the entire city and seemed to intensify the suspense of my upcoming expedition. 1957 seemed to have brought in a rash of inclement weather including four straight days of steady rain prior to my departure. My mother held my hand as we walked on the slippery cobblestones toward the train station realizing that this may be my last stroll down Breite Strasse. The coal burning stoves heating the nearby homes generated their usual brown exhaust that blended in with the surrounding fog creating a dismally heavy cloud that hung over the streets. Smoke coming from the chimneys hung in the air as though held in suspension by the fog.

The first leg of my journey consisted of taking the four o'clock train that afternoon to Oschersleben. A thirty-minute train ride directly north of Quedlinburg. I received very skimpy information regarding the next steps in order to preserve the secrecy of the escape route. I knew that a series of evasive maneuvers were planned but had been purposely kept in the dark.

We arrived at the Quedlinburg train station an hour early, as I wanted to be certain I wouldn't be late. A frightful nervousness gripped my mother as we waited outside the station. She had spent enough time in jail as a guest of the East German government and had no desire for a return visit. Mommy made clumsy attempts to appear unconcerned and avoid looking suspicious. She thought that her whistling popular tunes along with a stream of distinctly forced laughter from time to time during our conversations would make our being there look quite innocent. In doing so, she actually appeared even more suspect. Making sure to purchase a round-trip train ticket for me in order to avoid any further suspicion, she told me to keep the return portion as a souvenir. We both expressed the hope that I would never need it.

Trains in Germany have always been famous for their punctuality. However, with the advent of the Russian influence only the West German trains adhered to any schedules. As four o'clock came and went both Mommy and I began to get somewhat nervous. My train was scheduled to connect to another train in Oschersleben going to Schoeningen, the next leg of my route. What if I missed the connection and was stuck in Oschersleben? I started to think about the consequences of being caught in the middle of some strange village by the police, who would wonder what possessed me to wear three sets of underwear, and two layers of outer clothing. In fact, I knew it wouldn't take them long to figure out what was going on. Meanwhile, the rain and fog continued as darkness started to close in on us.

At last, the train arrived an hour late, by which time both my mother and I had become nervous wrecks in our attempts to look casual. During our final two hours together we had talked mostly about Pappi, Erich, and Rosel, being very careful to avoid the sensitive issues that had driven us apart. As I climbed onto the rail car being careful to not make it look like this would be a long separation, I kissed her good-bye. No long hugs or embraces. With all of the people milling around the station, some certain to be informers, as well as the men in leather coats, obviously Stasi, it had to appear as though I would be returning the next morning. With a sense of adventure, I boarded the train not knowing whether or not I would ever see any of my family again. The journey had officially begun.

While riding the short stretch to Oschersleben, I was far too nervous to read the magazines I'd brought with me, and tried to remember the next phase of the excursion. It called for changing trains in Oschersleben and connecting with the commuter train to Schoeningen. There I would meet Munser after another thirty kilometer ride. Each leg of the journey put me closer to the border. Concerned about his own security, he told me to wear a flower in my lapel to indicate my certainty that no one had followed me. Because of my love of flowers, I determined not to wear anything artificial and packed three or four homegrown roses loosely in the overnight bag that never left my side.

Fortunately, the connecting train from Oschersleben to Schoeningen arrived late, giving time to wander around the Oschersleben station by myself. Between the darkening sky, the depressingly bone chilling drizzle, and the dropping temperatures I felt that I was the subject of a Stephen King mystery novel living in some sort of supernatural world.

I walked outside the station and looked at the homes nestled in the nearby neighborhood streets. Darkened by years of brown coal fumes that had permanently stained the white plaster, each home told its own story. As I walked on the wet slimy cobblestones occasionally losing my footing in the darkness, I tried to look in the windows of the few homes that had lights glowing inside. The narrow darkened street permitted me to walk directly down the center and see through the windows on both sides. Now and then I could see a face looking back at me before they quickly pulled down the shades. For all they knew I could have been a Stasi investigator. The emptiness of the streets, void of any activity by either people or cars, provided quietness that was almost sinister.

The homes strongly resembled those in Quedlinburg with their half-timbered vertical beams surrounded with plaster soiled by the brown smoke constantly floating from the chimneys. They stood tall and narrow with common walls joining them together providing no space for grassy yards between houses. Those instances where I saw people in their firelit but Spartan living rooms provided me with opportunities to make up stories imagining how they lived their lives and whether or not they would be alive next year.

By nine o'clock I returned to the station and wondered whether I looked suspicious to the men roaming around the station in their leather coats. Being somewhat closer to the border now, the number of Stasi had increased as they intensified their efforts to prevent people like me from crossing. One of them actually approached me to question my presence there alone at this hour. This short stubby little man in his menacing leather overcoat looked at me like he had cornered a thief who had stolen the crown jewels. His look seemed to bore a hole right through my brain as he stared directly into my eyes. I can't describe the panic that raced through the pit of my stomach as I very casually told him that I planned to visit a friend in Schoeningen.

If he had asked for the name of the friend or her address, I honestly don't think I would be writing this story today, as I had no answer. It would have been a very quick and nasty trip to the police station, and from there to some prison for interrogation. Fortunately, we both heard the train whistle at the same time and I picked up my bag and headed onto the platform before he could pursue the subject any further. All I could think of was that my freedom had come to an end, and my mother and brother would eventually suffer as well.

As I boarded the train for Schoeningen, I noticed that my interrogator remained behind on the platform, either to harass the next group of passengers, or to simply keep an eye out for anyone looking with a suspicious glint of potential freedom in their eyes. I couldn't get his mean, chubby face out of my mind as the train gradually pulled out making its way to Schoeningen and my walk through the deadly minefields.

After an uneventful ride to Schoeningen I departed the train and reached into my purse to retrieve the rose. By now it had wilted, but was still recognizable. I probably should have alerted Munser about my encounter with the Stasi at the Oschersleben train platform, but I had no intention at this point to create any doubts in his mind that might delay my escape. As far as anyone was concerned, no one had followed me or become suspicious of my movements.

As I left the train, I immediately spotted Munser talking on the platform with another elderly couple in their mid-fifties. They too had flowers in their lapels. It appeared that I would have company on my expedition.

As I approached the three of them, Munser saw me coming and put his fingers to his lips motioning me to be silent. I said nothing as he gestured for the three of us to follow him into the station. As the local church bells pealed the midnight hour, we followed him through the building, but rather than going out of the main entrance, he motioned for the three of us to leave through the side door exiting on to the street. We assumed that he would meet us outside as he headed alone for the main exit.

As we walked out into the cold wet sidewalk next to the train station, a sweeping number of second thoughts overwhelmed me. Who was this other couple? Could this guy Munser really be trusted? Now that he had our money, what would prevent him from simply walking away and leaving us in the miserably damp midnight weather of a town I had never seen?

The side door of the station led to a dismally unlit alley, and the darkened homes I saw in the distance spewed forth the usual brown smoke that continued to hang in the air. An occasional man in a leather coat would walk by the entrance to the alley, and I held on to the woman who brusquely motioned for me to be quiet and let go of her coat. I now became very frightened after realizing the possible consequences if Munser never showed up again.

As my eyes became accustomed to the dark, I could make out a hay wagon hooked on to a tractor parked in the alley about thirty meters from the station door. After a tense few minutes I finally saw Munser round the corner into the alley. Without saying a word, he motioned us to board the hay wagon, lie down, and cover ourselves with the drenched straw. I remember clawing down to the wooden platform of the wagon in order to pile as much of the wet straw as possible to conceal my body.

We listened to his instructions and, after lying in the wagon for a few minutes, it began to move ever so slowly. By now fear and freezing cold had gripped all of my senses. Even though I wore three layers of clothing, the bitter damp air cut right through everything and chilled my insides. I couldn't stop shivering but took some comfort in the fact that I could hear the older gentleman who was with us shaking more than I.

The slow and bumpy ride lasted about thirty minutes, having lost all track of time by now. When we stopped I opened my eyes for the first time since boarding the wagon. I could see nothing but an open field surrounded by dense woods with just enough moonlight for Munser to point out the watchtower being manned by one of the East German police or Russian soldiers. I never did know whom to fear the most.

Then he spoke the first words I had heard from him all night. Very concisely he stated that we must be extremely quiet and say absolutely nothing. He told us that we would crawl through the farm field strewn with land mines, but if we stayed directly behind him we would be safe. As he pointed to the watchtower, he said that he had already bribed the guards with vodka the previous day and they wouldn't shoot even if they saw us. He expressed only one concern; it might not be the same guards on duty that night, so be very careful. How comforting!

He then pointed out a second tower a few hundred yards away where the powerful beam of a searchlight could be seen swinging back and forth across the fields and through the nearby woods. Munser said that if the light were to land on us we must come to a dead halt, not moving a single muscle. He sensed my nervousness and tried to comfort me by saying that he had done this on many occasions and had never once been caught.

Without wasting any more valuable time, he walked us through a narrow section of the farm field to the nearby forest. When we reached a short stubby pine tree that I believe he used as his guidepost, he motioned for us to get down on our hands and knees and begin the long crawl through the woods to freedom. Being the youngest, I remained directly behind Munser. The older woman followed me with the man, I assumed to be her husband, bringing up the rear. By this time my mind had grown numb from the overload of fear and tension that controlled my entire thinking process. My body responded automatically to Munser's directions, realizing that if I had stopped to analyze the possible dangers that lay ahead I would have frozen with panic.

I never really knew anything about the other couple, or even if they were married, as we never spoke one word from the time we first saw each other until the final hour when we went our separate ways. For all I knew, they could have been Stasi informers, and they may certainly have thought the same of me. Such was the climate in East Germany. You could never go wrong saying as little as possible to both friends and strangers, since virtually no one could be trusted. Little wonder that I was so anxious to flee.

As I crawled through the long wet field grass and felt the muddy earth soak through my three layers of clothing, my mind conjured up all kinds of peculiar thoughts. I couldn't help but think back on the number of times that I had come home from school as a little girl caked with mud on dresses my mother had recently sewn. How upset she had been when I walked in the door after a hard day of playing in the dirty puddles or climbing trees wearing one of those new dresses. What would she say now, knowing that every stitch of clothing I owned oozed with the filth and muck of the border zone's "no man's land?"

More reflections danced around in my head during that long and tedious crawl. Some of them took the tension out of the drudgery, and others reminded me of the fact that I may never return to this part of the world again. A world that held so many memories of a childhood wrought with war, death, imprisonment, and distrust.

A few pleasant memories of things I would be leaving behind also crept into my mind such as the teachers who had instilled within me a botanical insight and appreciation of the flowering garden. They taught me how to love and nurture the blossoming plants that today have become my most precious pastime. I fondly recollected my sports companions who accompanied me to so many events throughout the country. Yes, we competed with each other as well as the opposing teams and certainly got into our share of mischief. But we always stood by each other and provided the moral support when one of us was overcome with defeat.

Most of all I thought about the unique beauty of my home in the midst of the magnificent Harz Mountains. Would I ever again walk the narrow mountain paths that Rosel and I had meandered outside of Quedlinburg or even visit the Market Square of my city nestled so comfortably between the shimmering mountain peaks? Would I ever again ride a bicycle on the trails where I blindly followed Pappi on those warm Sunday afternoons? Probably not but, on balance, the evil I was escaping far outweighed the good, and I was more than contented to be departing.

Before becoming overpowered by a futile wave of nostalgia, I had to refocus on the mission at hand which meant staying close behind Munser.

The first time one of the bright beams of the tower spotlights hit me I froze lying face down in the mud. All the daydreaming that had been going on in my head came abruptly to an end and I quickly returned to reality. After the seventh or eighth time it became routine. Realizing that we were nearly halfway, a feeling of exhilaration slowly crept into my stomach with the expectation of a new life ahead of me.

The rain continued to fall sporadically and the cold air penetrated my body unmercifully, but the anticipation drove me, as well as my elderly cohorts, towards our destination.

It must have been close to two hours later that our faithful guide, Munser, stood up and quietly chuckled, "You may all stand up and walk like human beings again. You are now in West Germany." At first, my mind had a difficult time grasping the depth of his statement. But, after two hours of groping on my hands and knees and crawling on my stomach, I felt excited just to be able to walk again.

As I took my first steps the thought of Munser's comment began to sink in. I cried uncontrollably and the harder I tried to stop, the more my sobbing persisted. I don't, to this day, understand what caused this reaction. It might have been a combination of feelings that had continued to build within me during the past several months or even years. But when I stopped I truly felt refreshed.

Just prior to dawn breaking, I could make out another figure approaching us from a distance. Munser told us that this would be our guide to the local train station from where we could go our separate ways. He wanted to make certain that he re-crossed the border immediately ahead of the rising sun. With no further words spoken he turned to go back and no contact has ever been made by either of us again. I'm certain that this was intentional for his own security as well as ours.

Our new guide, a tall lanky fellow with a much gentler face than Munser's, sported more western style clothing. His jeans fit snugly under a denim jacket and his athletic shoes gave him the appearance of coming straight out of a men's outdoor hunting magazine. I would actually categorize him as one of the more handsome gentleman I had ever met, although the stubble on his face indicated he'd gone three or four days without shaving. He couldn't have been over thirty years old and expressed a great deal of enthusiasm in assuming his duties of getting us underway.

According to our new guide, whose name I never did know, we had arrived at the outskirts of Helmstedt. This city had become one of the main border crossing checkpoints separating East and West, manned by American soldiers on one side and Russians on the other. Between the two guard posts was a space of fifty to a hundred meters known as "No Man's Land," not a good place to be spending any time. The law required that all traffic travelling between West Germany and Berlin drive through Helmstedt on the Autobahn, the primary traffic conduit passing through this location. Both guard points stopped every vehicle going in either direction to check for valid passports and other required documentation. This process frequently took over an hour as the Russians intentionally employed it as a means of hassling West German citizens and American soldiers.

Standing in the middle of this dreary farmer's field as dawn began to break I could see in the distance the Helmstedt city lights and could vaguely make out the shadows of some of the taller buildings. The sight of streetlights in the distance was exhilarating and in such contrast to cities in the East. As our new guide walked us the mile or two to the train station, my excitement and sense of freedom blocked out the chill from the continuing bitter cold drizzle. My small overnight suitcase seemed so much lighter than it had before.

He handed me a train ticket that would take me to the city of Pirmasens in southern Germany. Apparently, the money that my mother had paid to Munser had covered not only his fee, but also the fee for our new guide, and the cost of this ticket. The process of smuggling East Germans out of their distressed circumstances had obviously become a well synchronized business. It involved a chain of contacts that coordinated not only the trips through the minefields, but the bribing of watchtower guards and agents in the West who made the necessary travel arrangements.

Why Pirmasens? First of all, it would have been far too dangerous for me to take the train to Rosel in West Berlin, my ultimate destination. I would have had to travel back across the border and ride the 200 kilometers through East Germany to get there. Papers would have to be checked and rechecked as the train ride progressed. The attendants and their police escorts would be asking all sorts of questions, as to how a young lady got from Quedlinburg to Helmstedt, and why was she headed for Berlin.

Secondly, Pirmasens happened to be where Rosel's and Mommy's old friend, David Warshamsky, had resettled after closing up his black market business in Berlin. He had used his profits to buy a popular restaurant and cocktail lounge in a city heavily populated with American soldiers. Obviously, he had a nose for money and knew how to invest it. He had also been contacted by Rosel to provide some temporary shelter for her younger sister, me.

By the time we reached the train station in Helmstedt the rising sun of dawn broke through the clouds and the rain had ceased. I took this as an omen of good fortune since the past four days had provided nothing but a cold wet cloud covering. Chilled to the bone and totally exhausted, having lived through one of the most unforgettable nights of my life, I bathed in my freedom.

The couple that accompanied me during the long night boarded a train heading north, and I simply waved good-bye, with neither of us uttering a word. I waited for the train going to Frankfurt. From there I would connect to Kaiserslautern and eventually to Pirmasens.

During the uneventful train ride, I realized that I looked like a complete disaster with my dirty and torn clothing, certain that the other passengers recognized me for what I was, an escapee from the East. To be honest, my total exhaustion prevented me from caring what they thought as I slept most of the way to Frankfurt.

CHAPTER XXII
The New Beginning

In the meantime, my mother had been arranging for Erich's escape as well, and somehow made arrangements for him to travel to Heidelberg where many of his paintings were on display at one of the museums. As an artist he was much freer to travel across the border than technical personnel, young people, or athletes. The Communist mentality in those days focused on the pragmatic aspects of human life not the artistic.

My mother devised a rather complex set of plans, now that I think back on it. She had instructed me to remain in Pirmasens a few weeks with David Warshamsky while Erich went to Heidelberg to stay with an old friend. She in turn planned to leave Quedlinburg two weeks later packing some very simple belongings and taking the train to Berlin for a routine visit with Rosel. Not many questions would be asked of a fifty seven-year-old lady carrying a small canvas overnight bag on her way to see her daughter. At her age, there was no problem going directly to Berlin, as the older people with no particular skills were considered a liability by the East Germans, and were free to escape at will. Eventually Erich and I were to coordinate with Rosel and meet at her apartment in Berlin once Mommy had arrived.

So much for the best laid plans. Only three days had passed since my departure before acquaintances began asking my mother why they hadn't seen Barbara around the neighborhood. They started asking about Erich as well. It didn't take her long to get the message. She immediately packed her bags and headed for Berlin by train. Her real concern was the possibility that she might suffer the consequences once they had discovered that Erich and I were gone.

That was the last the Russians and the East German police would ever see of Margarete Spannaus and last that my mother would ever see of her home on Breite Strasse. With the departure of my mother from Quedlinburg, the last Spannaus to inhabit "The Breite

Strasse House" had left forever. The house that had been in our family for over 420 years had been abandoned along with all of its furniture and contents. As I related earlier, during my last visit in 1999, I wept as I stood on the corner viewing the main entrance all boarded up, along with many of the windows that had already been shattered.

Arriving at the Pirmasens train station, with a horrendous cold and just enough West German marks for a taxi, I asked the driver to take me to Warshamky's Atlantic Bar and Restaurant. Not certain how welcome I would be, I realized that I had no other choice at this point other than to rely upon my mother's former black market partner for refuge.

As I rode in the taxi from the train station to the Atlantic Bar I couldn't help but notice the large number of American soldiers milling around in the streets. Being Sunday meant that most of them were off duty and taking advantage of a very lively city. The vitality so visible in this West German town contrasted dramatically with cities in the East Zone. People walked in and out of local shops carrying packages with their latest purchases and seemed to glide down the sidewalks rather than trudging along as they did on the other side of the border. I then knew how Dorothy felt when arrived in the land of OZ.

Uncle David, as I now referred to him, immediately showed me to my bedroom over the restaurant. Without even bothering to undress or clean up, I lay down on the bed and slept for two straight days. I realized that my journey had been only partially completed.

After two or three weeks with no opportunity to make friends in Pirmasens, I began to get very lonely. I helped in the restaurant where I could, in order to keep busy, but anxiously looked forward to getting to Berlin to rejoin my family. Finally, after another week in Pirmasens, Rosel sent me the plane ticket to Berlin so I could rejoin my family. At last I would have the opportunity to reunite with Rosel, who I missed so very much, along with Erich and Mommy. It had been such a long time since the four of us had lived together.

Upon arriving in Berlin, there were some additional procedures that had to be followed which applied to all escapees seeking refuge in West Berlin. It began with my mother and I having to report to a type of refugee camp operated jointly by the American, British, and French military. The camp itself consisted of a large open area fenced in on all sides. It looked more like a deserted military base that probably billeted some of Hitler's former troops during the war. Inside the compound a number of three story brick barracks housed several of the other refugees and detainees who had no other place to live.

The American official responsible for our family required us to register and undergo an interrogation process lasting on and off for about two weeks. Fortunately, the camp's proximity to Rosel's apartment permitted us to return home each night where we could sit around her small living room exchanging experiences encountered during our individual migrations to Berlin. Those refugees with no other place to stay resided in the camp until they could find a means of support and some sort of private living quarters.

My former membership in the Free German Youth and Young Pioneers seemed to stump most of our interrogators. They knew of their Communist origin as youth indoctrination organizations, but seemed unaware that youngsters my age had no choice but to join them. They found it difficult to understand that I didn't apply for acceptance. The State simply enrolled me and instructed me to attend meetings. We were conscripted primarily for the purpose of attending all demonstrations when the Communist big whigs came to town so we could wave flags and cheer them on to greater things. The Americans, I imagine, compared it to the Hitler Youth and probably thought I had the potential of becoming a dangerous subversive. It only took two weeks to convince them otherwise. Even though going to the interrogation center each day proved to be somewhat of a hassle, they did provide us a per diem amount of money with which to buy food and pay for transportation. Since we lived within walking distance, we simply used the transportation allowance to buy extra food. Eventually, we received official papers indicating our Berlin citizenship.

So there I was, nineteen years old, free to pursue whatever I wanted to do, and feeling as though the weight of the world had been lifted from my shoulders. What's more, I could say what I thought to anyone, without fear of imprisonment. Unless you've lived on the other side of the border you simply wouldn't be able to understand or appreciate the feeling of freedom and independence that accompanies this liberation.

My first major decision involved going to an employment agency to find a job. We all needed the money. Between the agency and the newspaper want ads I came across an employment opportunity with Siemens Electronics. Their factory needed an assembly line worker to solder printed circuit boards. I was their girl. I knew that this would be temporary, as my determination to find something using my talents in the field of botany would eventually uncover something more challenging.

Erich, meanwhile, had moved to Heidelberg and became terribly unhappy. He couldn't get used to the idea of being totally independent of the State and knew that to survive he would have to perform magic with his paintings. As it turned out, he did manage to earn a living from his art. Not an extravagant living, but enough to provide food and shelter.

Life had become fairly routine for Rosel, Mommy, and I, to the point that carelessness nearly cost me my freedom. Along with Rosel's child, Beate, we lived in a confined one-bedroom apartment where life became rather stifling. From time to time I just wanted to get out by myself. At that time Germany had two currencies, the West German mark equaled four East German marks. The prices, however, in East Berlin weren't four times more expensive than in the West. To have my hair styled in West Berlin cost twelve West marks while in East Berlin it cost twelve East Marks, the equivalent of only three West marks. Therefore, things cost much less for those of us who had West German marks to spend in the East. It didn't take me long to figure out that, with very little effort, I could take the U-Bahn back and forth between East and West Berlin and go to the beauty shop in the East for one fourth the cost of having my hair done in the West.

Thinking that my newly acquired West Berlin citizenship papers acted as a protective shield, I made this trip routinely on a weekly basis. Unaware of the fact that our family name was listed in a thick leather book held by each Stasi agent, I found my trips to East Berlin somewhat of a getaway from our cramped living quarters. The Stasi kept meticulous records of every individual who somehow escaped their grasp.

After my fourth or fifth shopping trip to East Berlin, I stood on the platform waiting for the U-Bahn to take me back home. A rather short stocky man in a leather coat approached me, and I immediately recognized him as Stasi. He held a thick leather bound book in his hands as he asked me for my papers. It only took him a minute to find the name Spannaus in his book and, without any explanation, told me to follow him.

At this point, my mind reeled with panic, as I thought of the sheer stupidity of my being in this situation. My mother had spent all of our money to get me out of this appalling country, and I had crawled through muck and slimy fields strewn with land mines to escape, and now, on my own accord, I returned for the sake of saving a few marks. I had reached the epitome of sheer idiocy.

We walked to a police car and drove to a local prison for my interrogation. For twelve solid hours they asked me all sorts of questions regarding my family and friends. How did I get to West Berlin and obtain citizenship papers? Where was Frau Spannaus, my mother, and Erich Spannaus? Where in Berlin did I live? What happened to some other friends of mine that formerly lived in Quedlinburg? How did I get the money to travel back and forth?

In a state of total panic and frustration my only response consisted of sobbing and telling them how sorry I felt for being there. Every hour or two they sent me to a small back room with no windows to think about elaborating upon my responses. That didn't help much since my state of turmoil didn't allow me to think all that clearly. After spending about fifteen minutes in the back room they returned me to the interrogation cell with the bright lights and continued the questioning. Finally, the police felt that I would be of very little use to them, and my immature behavior convinced them to release me.

By midnight they put me out on the street and pointed to the nearest U-Bahn station. I arrived home at about two o'clock in the morning to find my mother crying outside the apartment in a state of frenzy. No one had called to tell her that I'd been detained and, because she had known that I was going into the East Zone, she thought the worst. I had embarked on a senseless venture to save a few marks. Never again.

My Escape from East Germany

CHAPTER XXIII
An American Enters My Life

As life returned to an almost normal state, if such a thing existed in the Germany of the 1950's, I continued living with my mother, Rosel, and Rosel's seven-year-old daughter. We still crowded into our tiny one-bedroom apartment, which had become a bit roomier now that Erich was living in Heidelberg. It meant that both the kitchen and living room became sleeping quarters at night. Rosel and Beate shared the twin bedroom, Mommy slept on the pullout couch in the living room and I made do on the small couch nestled in the corner of the kitchen. Of course, Erich visited from Heidelberg, from time to time, to grumble about his own living conditions in Southern Germany, and bemoan the fact that Mommy had coerced him to evacuate the comforts of the Communist state. His visits merely added to our overcrowded situation as he slept in the twin bedroom forcing Rosel and Beate to share one of the small beds.

Taking a bath in those living quarters also proved to be a challenging experience. It meant taking the coal bucket down four flights of stairs to the apartment cellar, filling it to the weight that could be hauled back up without breaking one's back, and filling the oven to heat the water. As a result the luxury of bathing became a rarity.

My mother had been searching for another apartment during this period so that she and I could get a little more space and allow Rosel and Beate more privacy; however, the lengthy waiting list in our complex prevented us from moving.

A few months later, in order to relieve the overcrowded living conditions, as well as bring additional income into the household, my mother traveled to Pirmasens to become a full-time chef in David Warshamsky's Atlantic Bar and Restaurant. This left Rosel, Beate and I a bit more room to spread out. Warshamsky felt partially responsible for Mommy's previous incarceration, and because he now had become almost part of the family he not only provided work for her but living quarters over the restaurant. As I related earlier, this establishment eventually played an important role in my life.

During the Fasching season of February 1958, Mommy asked Rosel and I to come south to visit her for a few days in Pirmasens. Fasching is the German version of Mardi Gras and is celebrated in southern Germany with the same level of enthusiasm and intensity as Mardi Gras in New Orleans. Some who have experienced both festivals think Fasching to be even more intense.

After a few days in Pirmasens I began preparing for my return to Berlin and my job at Siemens. The Tuesday night before Ash Wednesday Rosel, Mommy, and I were having dinner together in the restaurant while the band played dance music in the next room. The interior was set up like a nightclub with a bar running the entire length of one wall in the room where the band played with cocktail tables interspersed around the dance floor. In the dining area adjacent to the dance floor we were finishing a late dinner. The entire place was packed with local Germans and American soldiers in civilian clothes.

We had just finished our desert when one of the Americans, looking somewhat lost, casually walked by our table as though he were looking for the men's room. He approached from the bar section that I knew contained a clearly marked men's room which he apparently chose to ignore. Obviously, not looking to relieve himself, he clumsily, without really stopping, asked me in mid-stride if I would care to dance. He seemed fearful of being rejected and, by not formally stopping to ask, it wouldn't appear quite as embarrassing if I turned him down. Actually, as I discovered much later, he had made a bet with another one of the officers that he could get me to dance with him.

I had turned down every proposal to dance since I'd been in Pirmasens, so both Rosel and Mommy were greatly surprised that I had so readily accepted his offer. To be very honest, the American, I believe, was just as astonished as they were. He introduced himself as David Bloomfield, an "officer" in the

United States Army. As though I couldn't have guessed.

As we danced to the Louie Armstrong version of "Blueberry Hill" he proceeded to ask me the usual questions guys ask girls when they don't know what else to talk about. It took him a few minutes of rambling on before he realized that I didn't speak a word of English and understood even less. I spoke only German and the Russian that we were forced to learn in school, none of which he understood.

In attempting to explain that I had recently escaped from East Germany, I could see that everything I said sailed right over his head. I finally found the right words to trigger a reaction. In explaining that I came from the Russian zone, he immediately picked up on the word "Ruskie." With that, he interpreted that I must be Russian and immediately assumed I might be some sort of spy. He had recently arrived in Germany and naively thought that his rank and security clearance would make him the target of all sorts of espionage agents. That nearly ended the dance in mid-stream. I could see his consternation until I somehow got the message across that, no, I was not Russian but had escaped from the Russian zone.

We danced to the music of a host of songs popular in the 50's, when both my mother and sister indicated that my bedtime had arrived. Both were quick to remind me that I had an early train to catch in the morning. They were really saying "If you know what's good for you, you'll stay away from the Ami's," as American soldiers were nicknamed during the occupation. I must admit, that in spite of their warning, I really enjoyed myself with David, as we carried on a conversation using hand signals and words easily translated between German and English.

After Rosel's repeated attempts to bring an end to this tryst with the American taking place on the dance floor and at our dinner table, David and I agreed to exchange addresses and correspond with each other. In order to avoid being seen by Mommy as we exchanged addresses we slipped outside. On this very clear night David, in his effort to show off his knowledge of astronomy, pointed out the constellation Orion. To this day Orion serves as my "favorite talisman" and we always seek him out on starry nights. When I returned inside, Mommy hurried me off to bed and David returned to his comrades to collect his winnings from the bet.

Our letters between Berlin and Pirmasens, interestingly enough, became the fuel that ignited David's desire to visit Berlin. Neither of us had previously spent much time corresponding with anyone, let alone a perfect stranger with whom we'd spent a total of only two hours. For some unknown reason, the letter writing became almost obsessive. Each time I received one I could hardly wait to sit down and compose the reply. David apparently did the same. There was no point in conversing by phone as neither of us could speak the other's language. Of course, his letters, all in English, required translation, so I took them to a lady fluent in both languages in the downstairs apartment. She read and translated them for me while we sat at her kitchen table. David took my letters to one of the chefs at the Pirmasens officers club who did the same. I suppose both of our translators learned an awful lot about us during the course of the next eighteen months.

One day I received a note saying that he really wanted to visit me in Berlin. He used the excuse that he would love to see the city about which he'd heard so much and asked if I could help him find his way around, or even be his guide. I admit that I was stunned but highly flattered. At first I hesitated to encourage this visit as he had no idea of our cramped living conditions and hoped that he had no plans to spend the few days as our house guest. It would have meant sleeping in the bathtub.

Fortunately, David made arrangements to reside at the bachelor officers quarters in Dahlem, a suburb of Berlin that served as the headquarters of the American occupying forces.

We spent the entire week going from one historic sight to another, while he took hundreds of pictures on his new camera. We drove in his little Renault Dauphine from the Seigessäule, a towering spire adorned by a golden statue on it's peak overlooking the city, to the Funkturm, Berlin's tallest structure serving as its radio broadcasting tower. We then hurried off to see the famous Brandenburg Gate, the structure inspired by the Acropolis in Athens, which divided East and West Berlin.

Not far from the Brandenburg Gate was the Soviet monument, where a Russian soldier ceremoniously guarded an armored tank placed on a magnificent marble edifice. He obviously had strict instructions to remain silent and stoic when visitors came, but my adventurous nature required David to take pictures of me pretending to carry on a conversation with him. I finally got him to crack a smile that could have placed him in serious trouble if witnessed by the East block authorities.

When standing on the top steps of the monument, we could see the Reichstag, once the seat of the German parliament, still gutted by a fire ordered by Hitler in his attempt to destroy crucial documents and seize control of the government. It remained a burned out edifice since the Russians had little desire to perform any restorations. Although we didn't visit East Berlin at that time, it wasn't difficult to look across the border dividing the city to witness the state of disrepair maintained by the Russian and East German authorities.

David couldn't get enough sightseeing done in the time frame he allowed for his visit and became fascinated with each famous structure and landmark taking picture after picture. Using a city map we wound our way through the streets of Berlin getting lost more frequently than he would have liked. He became angry with me each time we lost our way thinking that I was a native of Berlin, thereby expecting me to know the city like the back of my hand. He didn't stop to realize that I had lived there less than a year with no car so this became my first opportunity to see many of these historic monuments.

It amazed us both how we could walk hand in hand down the Kurfürstendamm laughing and talking, mostly using hand gestures to communicate, and so thoroughly enjoy being alive and with each other. He brought with him a German/English, English/German dictionary that, by the end of the week, was in tatters it had been used so much. We sat over ice cream dishes served by fashionable outdoor cafes carrying on conversations in sign language while flipping through the pages of the dictionary, somehow learning to understand each other. Meanwhile, he was taking German classes in Pirmasens, which he seemed to be mastering quite well.

After three days of exhausting driving from one historic site to the next, we decided to spend a relaxing day enjoying the Berlin Zoo. Both of us loved animals and appreciated their roaming around in very naturally constructed habitats.

That night David somehow obtained front row balcony seats at the famous Berlin Opera House to see Carmen. This turned out to be one of the more embarrassing evenings of my life. I wore my finest dress that had taken Mommy days to sew and David wore his ten-year-old sport jacket with a glaringly loud tie. The other male opera attendees were in tuxedos or formal dark suits. Halfway through the first act David placed his feet up on the railing of the balcony to get comfortable. I started to become disillusioned with the American culture if this was any indication. The crusher came when, shortly after the feet went up, I heard the sound of snoring from a sleeping David sitting next to me. I couldn't have been more humiliated.

During David's last few days we continued our search for Berlin's monuments visiting Charlottenburg Palace with its Museum of Decorative Arts, the Olympic Stadium built by Hitler for the 1936 Olympic Games, and the new and very modern Congress Hall in the Tiergarten area. We marveled at the Kaiser Wilhelm Memorial Church, referred to by most as the "Symbol of Berlin," built in the late eighteen hundreds and nearly completely destroyed by the bombing of Berlin during World War II. The bombed out structure still remains standing as the focal point among the fashionable hotels and restaurants on the Kurfürstendamm.

Finally, I took David to the heart of prewar Berlin's Jewish district where we visited the synagogue so badly damaged during the infamous Kristallnacht. Needless to say, neither of us spoke but he fought hard to hold back his tears.

After spending an entire week together from breakfast time until he brought me home each night, it became clear to me that we had fallen seriously in love despite the language barrier that we somehow managed to overcome. I felt quite certain that David's feelings echoed mine.

During the first several months of our romance we continued to visit each other in Pirmasens and Berlin and neither of us had any idea where the relationship was headed. I'm sure that if either of our parents had an inkling as to how seriously we felt towards each other, they would have made every effort to bring the relationship to an abrupt halt. In short, the thought of explaining to my mother that I had fallen in love with a Jewish man, after fifteen years of her indoctrination by Hitler and the Nazi Party would have been futile. David's parents, on the other hand, would have never even suspected that he would dare to bring a German bride into his home. Their feelings towards Germans following two world wars and a Holocaust was nothing short of scorn.

A year after our first meeting in Pirmasens David took a command assignment in Ulm, Germany, closer to the Bavarian border and only a two-hour drive from Heidelberg. Being an opportunist, I told Mommy that I would like to move to Heidelberg to be near Erich and, at the same time, practice my profession of horticulture in one of the many nurseries situated in that part of Germany. Not at all deceived, she knew very quickly that my motives had nothing to do with Erich and growing flowers. My being 21 at the time meant that she could do very little to prevent my moving south, and she had resigned herself to the fact that her daughter had fallen in love with an American Jew. She could swallow the American part of the equation, but the Jewish aspect really tried her patience.

I found a family in the Heidelberg suburb of Edingen who had a small room to rent, not far from the nursery that employed me. They owned a modest home situated on the banks of the Neckar River that flowed through the heart of the city. When David came to visit each weekend, we often sat on the bluffs overlooking the river as we struggled to resolve the direction and future of our relationship. By this time, he had successfully learned to communicate passably in German, and had been moderately successful in teaching me a basic English vocabulary.

We enjoyed all that Heidelberg had to offer including the wondrous castle overlooking the river and the restaurants where David invariably ordered his favorite dish, weinerschnitzel. At night we enjoyed walking the streets listening to the college students from the famous Heidelberg University raising their beer steins in the local pubs as they sang one German song after another. David said it always reminded him of the operetta, "The Student Prince." Occasionally I took the train to Ulm to visit him on the weekends he served as duty officer for the army base.

These visits continued for about six months, at which time David's schedule called for his transfer back to the United States with his tour of military duty quickly approaching closure. One evening shortly before his departure, as we sat on the grass by our favorite spot on the Neckar riverbank, the discussion again led to the question of our future. David stated that the time had arrived for conclusive action and real commitments without the luxury of the fantasy conversations to which we had always reverted in the past. Although he very decisively asked me that night to come to America to become his wife, I felt he had been caught up by the moment and the very romantic setting while not really believing that this could ever proceed to reality.

This guy who appeared from nowhere had apparently given little or no thought during the past eighteen months to the obstacles that could obstruct such a marriage. Was I expected to give up my country, my family, and my religion (which I never really did take that seriously), to move to a land of complete strangers? Not only strangers, but also a Jewish community that, most likely, would not provide the most affectionate welcome to a German Gentile while memories of the Holocaust and World War II remained fresh in their minds. David had always felt strongly about his Jewish background and stipulated that his proposal depended upon my conversion to Judaism. I could just see my mother responding to this one. My father, had he been alive, would never have permitted the relationship to even progress this far, but if it had, the final condition of conversion would have created another world war.

As we sat on the bluffs watching the night sky darken, our discussion became more and more intense. At first I thought that David wanted to express his parting words in such a way as to spare my feelings prior to his leaving Germany. After several hours his sincerity became more authentic, and I looked for a way to stall without making a firm commitment.

I realized that taking chances had become a large part of my history, and that I had risked a great deal in just escaping from East Germany. This proposal of marriage, however, required a great deal more thought than I had ever given to most matters in the past. Now, in the summer of 1959, I faced my closest companion's departure to another world in less than a month. In struggling to make a more rational decision, we agreed that he should plant his feet on the ground back in his home city of Shaker Heights, Ohio, for at least six months. I felt that this would give him the chance to reconsider all of the possible consequences of such a marriage and, at the same time, the opportunity to review the situation with his parents. I also felt that he needed the chance to revisit with some of his old girlfriends and, in doing so, might change his perspective on our relationship. I knew that living out of context for two years might distort some of his decision-making capabilities.

Also, where would my head be in six months? Would I really be willing to give up my family, my native country, and my religion to risk a completely new beginning with a group of foreigners? We both agreed that the waiting period was essential, regardless of the decision we reached at its conclusion

The Sunday evening of our last weekend together David boarded the train in Heidelberg destined for his new army base in Stuttgart, having been transferred there from Ulm for his final assignment. He had previously taken his car to the port at Bremerhaven for shipment back to the States and was limited to commuting by rail between our two cities for the past three weeks.

During that period we fell into a ritual of taking a taxi to the train station and walking around the "Bahnhof" area of Heidelberg for an hour or two before ordering dinner in the local station restaurant. He invariably ordered the large white bratwurst with French fries and German hard rolls, brotchen. He always joked about the fact that he really came to visit me on the weekends more for the bratwurst that seemed to be prepared in a very unique sauce.

On that last Sunday night we both lingered very quietly over dinner eating our meal without really tasting the food. Not a lot was said as we both knew that this might very well be the last time we would ever break bread together. We slowly walked out onto the train platform and, before walking up the steps to his car, he turned around and gave me a hug that nearly squeezed my insides all over the station platform. We were both holding back our tears, at least he seemed to be, as he boarded and took a window seat next to where I was standing. He seemed somewhat embarrassed as he reached into his pocket and grabbed some coins that he handed to me through the open window for my taxi fare home.

CHAPTER XXIV
The Path to America

Leaving the station that night as I walked toward the taxi stand, my thoughts were obviously confused. I felt grateful for the time we had spent together but was quite saddened by the fact that my chances of ever seeing David again were less than slim. I therefore made up my mind during the ride home that I would simply continue on with my life as a free West German happy to have escaped the oppression of the East.

From time to time I was quite surprised to receive letters from David, as I wasn't really sure that we would ever have any contact with each other again. We continued to correspond, however, during the next few months and since I had no access to a telephone, our communications were limited to the handwritten word. The most astonishing content of David's letters were his continual queries regarding the status of my application for a visa to come to the United States.

Could he really be serious? Did he think that I would now give up my newfound freedom, my family, my country, and possibly my religion on the whim that we could have one last fling together in America?

I certainly considered it; however, I knew that it was only a matter of time before David's mother would be guiding him in the direction of a "nice Jewish girl" to marry or at least divert his attention from the "German fräulein." In response to his constant questioning about why it was taking so long for me to get my papers to come to the States, I simply wrote him that my application had been submitted in October and here it was mid-December and I had heard nothing from the US Embassy. In fact, I had submitted no application to anyone. How sure was he that he really wanted me to come, and how sure was I that I really wanted to go? What happens if I go and we change our minds? Too much uncertainty.

In mid-January, totally stunned, I received a letter from the United States consulate in Berlin. They had received word from some Ohio congressman inquiring why the processing of my visa application took such an extraordinarily long time. They further stated that they had no such record of receiving my application and wanted to know the particulars.

Oh! Oh! David was really serious and I guess that letter served as the wake-up call to make me realize it. Having moved to Berlin by then in order to live with Mommy and Rosel, I took the streetcar to the US Embassy and proceeded to fill out a visa application for admission to the United States. Thus I committed right then and there to engage the wheels that would add a new adventure to a life that had already seen it's share of challenging exploits.

The letter from David's congressman provided the confirmation I needed to take the next step, but also added a new dimension of anxiety in my life which actually dwarfed the fear of crawling through the mine fields of East Germany.

CHAPTER XXV
The Arrival

My plane landed on March 7, 1961, in one of the worst snowstorms New York had ever seen. The flight may have been uneventful for most of the passengers, but for me it was one of sheer distress. For ten hours, which seemed more like ten days, I could think of nothing but the worst possible consequences taking place upon my arrival. David might not be there to meet me. His parents might turn their backs on me. What happens to someone getting off of a plane at New York's Laguardia Airport that can't speak a word of English and is simply left alone in the middle of the international terminal?

At that point I didn't want to find out. Having filled my mind with so many "what ifs," I refused to get off the plane. Finally, one of the flight attendants came to the rear of the airplane where I sat frozen to my seat and explained that "this is the end of the line." The cleaning crew would physically remove me unless I agreed to leave peacefully. David later told me that he felt he'd driven the twenty hours through a blinding snowstorm from Cleveland to New York in vain. He waited so long for me to enter the terminal that he assumed I had missed the plane.

I entered the passport control area and looked up to see a glassed in area two stories high, where those awaiting friends and family could look down to view the new arrivals. I nearly jumped out of my skin when I saw David standing there behind the glass waving frantically to get my attention.

After passing through passport control and customs, David was there to give me a hug that actually gripped me harder than the one he'd given me at the Heidelberg train station. Now I knew just how delighted he was to have me there. That didn't, however, relieve the tension in my stomach as to what was in store when I faced his parents.

I admit that I had no idea how to react to this sudden change of surroundings. A new country, a new life about to begin, and only one person in the entire world upon whom I could depend.

Still in a state of wonder, the two of us proceeded to pick up my luggage at the claim area and managed to lug it through the snow covered parking lot to David's tiny foreign car. He had purchased the Renault shortly before leaving Germany and shipped it back to the United States. An uncertain tenseness filled the air as we drove to the Ritz Carlton Hotel next to New York's famous Central Park.

While driving through the streets of New York City, which frequently reminded me of Berlin with all of its lighted buildings, traffic, and thousands of people scurrying around on the sidewalks, David unleashed a major surprise. I had been travelling for nearly twenty-four hours too excited to even close my eyes and nap for five minutes and could think of nothing I'd rather do now than go to a hotel room and sleep for two days. No! David's buddies from college and high school then living in the New York area had made plans for the weekend beginning that night.

Totally exhausted, I sat down on one of the cushy sofas in the Ritz Carlton Hotel lobby and dozed off while David checked in to the hotel. He had no idea how much of my energy this trip had consumed. He dragged me to the room and waited while I unpacked and showered. The shower actually restored some of my stamina and I perked up as I donned the frilly party dress my mom had sewn just before I left Berlin. I also looked forward to wearing the new white leather shoes Mommy had packed in my suitcase the day before. I will never forget the comments from one of the other women present that night about my being in New York and wearing white shoes in March. I had apparently committed a major violation of the American dress code.

We had been invited first to Jeffrey's apartment for cocktails where I met Harry, a law student at Harvard, Dick, a thriving industrialist who had taken over his father's business, Steve, a junior advertising executive, and Roger, who was still trying to "find himself." Of course, their wives and or girl friends accompanied them.

As David introduced me to each of his friends and their mates, all of whom came from wealthy suburban neighborhoods while attending Ivy League schools, I could think of only three things. One, these people had no concept of life's identity outside of their suburban social setting, two, I needed sleep in the worst way or I'd never get through the night, and three, why were these women so concerned about my wearing white shoes in March?

In spite of the electrifying intensity of the weekend, I fell in love with all of David's chums as well as most of their female companions. We dined at some of New York's upscale restaurants and breakfasted at the local lox and bagel delicatessens. I will always remember Harry taking me aside on the last day declaring that I was like a "breath of fresh air that had entered all of their lives."

We had broken the ice and the time had arrived to take the long drive in David's little Renault Dauphine from New York to Shaker Heights, over five hundred miles. As soon as we started driving out of the city my anxiety returned in spades, as I so greatly dreaded the inevitable meeting of David's parents in less than fifteen hours.

As David narrated about the wonders of our journey, the construction of the Lincoln Tunnel through which we passed, the history of the Pennsylvania Turnpike and the mountains through which the road tunneled, my mind could only focus on one thought. How would his devoted Jewish parents receive the daughter of a German army officer only fifteen years after the war between our countries had ended? I couldn't really concentrate on David's narration as I secretly hoped that the trip would never end.

The snow-covered roads slowed us down and it was midnight before we finally pulled into the Bloomfield driveway on Ludlow Road. I hoped my future in-laws would be sound asleep. Facing them at this hour could prove dangerous to my health.

David opened the side door to his home and both his mom and dad were there to greet me. It was a greeting I shall treasure for the rest of my life. With open arms they reached out to embrace and hug me and welcome me to their home and family. Never in my entire life had I felt such warmth and tenderness. Not even from my own mother and father.

I finally had a family.

My Escape from East Germany

EPILOGUE

It's been nearly 45 years, two children, and three grandchildren since David and I first met, and neither of us have regretted our decision.

We currently reside in Muskegon Michigan, where David has recently retired as president of a division of a major recreation company.

Our daughter, Shirley, serves as the vice president of the National Telephone Cooperative Association in Washington, DC. She lives in Arlington, Virginia with her husband Donald and our two wonderful granddaughters, Leah and Kelsey.

Our son, Jeremy, recently achieved his PHD in psychology while directing the rock climbing activities of the Chicagoland health clubs. He resides in Evanston, Illinois with his wife Christine and our lovely grandson, Joshua.

END

My Escape from East Germany

About the Author

David Bloomfield is an ex-US army officer stationed in Germany between 1957 and 1959, where he gathered the material for this book. Having married the central female character he became thoroughly familiar with the circumstances surrounding the Russian occupation of East Germany and the events leading up to his wife's escape. Mr. Bloomfield is currently a retired business executive living in Michigan.

LaVergne, TN USA
09 December 2009
166316LV00001B/5/A